NABOKOV AND
THE REAL WORLD

NABOKOV AND THE REAL WORLD

BETWEEN APPRECIATION
AND DEFENSE

ROBERT ALTER

PRINCETON UNIVERSITY PRESS

PRINCETON & OXFORD

Published by Princeton University Press
41 William Street, Princeton, New Jersey 08540
6 Oxford Street, Woodstock, Oxfordshire OX20 1TR

press.princeton.edu

All Rights Reserved
ISBN (pbk.) 978-0-691-21193-0
ISBN (e-book) 978-0-691-21866-3

Library of Congress Control Number: 2020951305

British Library Cataloging-in-Publication Data is available

Editorial: Anne Savarese, James Collier, and Jenny Tan
Production Editorial: Kathleen Cioffi
Text Design: Karl Spurzem
Cover Design: Chris Ferrante
Production: Erin Suydam
Publicity: Jodi Price and Amy Stewart
Copyeditor: Daniel Simon

Cover image: Detail of Karner Blue, *Lycaeides melissa samuelis*. Courtesy of USGSBIML Team

This book has been composed in Arno Pro

Printed on acid-free paper. ∞

Printed in the United States of America

10 9 8 7 6 5 4 3 2 1

For Hadas,
an avid reader at ten,
with many reading
pleasures ahead of her

CONTENTS

NABOKOV AND
THE REAL WORLD

1

Between Appreciation and Defense

Vladimir Nabokov (1899–1977) remains one of the most polarizing of the major novelists who have written in English. His admirers are passionate about him. These include both critics and many novelists in England, America, and elsewhere. Some gestures of imitation have been made by other writers, though as is generally the case with writers of the first order of originality—Proust and Kafka come to mind—these efforts have not been very successful. On the opposing side, there are some readers who cannot abide Nabokov, finding little in his work but coy literary devices, mannered or overwrought prose, and a pervasive archness. Such starkly antithetical responses are uncommon in the reception of eminent writers. Dickens, for example, may not be altogether to every reader's taste (Nabokov, as we shall see, happened to be keenly enthusiastic about him), and some may be put off by the gargoyle-like characters, the contrivances of plot, the bouts of sentimentality, yet by and large such readers might say they would rather read Jane Austen but are unlikely to consign Dickens to the dustbin of literature. That, however, is often what those who are put off by Nabokov have done.

In my own response as a critic to this polarization, the discussions that follow may strike some as a bit defensive. I avowedly do not assume that Nabokov is invariably at his best, that he is never free of the self-indulgence of which he is sometimes accused. But such accusation is often the result of a failure to see what is really going on in his novels, and my aim here is to show in a variety of finely tuned ways what such goings on entail. I should say that I have been writing about Nabokov for decades, and my basic view of him has not changed over the years, though it has been deepened by the exemplary work of his biographer and astute commentator, Brian Boyd, and by many critics, the first among them being his earliest prominent American critic, Alfred Appel Jr. Ever since I became an avid reader of Nabokov, I have been convinced that the self-reflexivity of his writing, its ingenious deployment of codes and games, its sheer literariness do not draw us away from the real world outside literature but, on the contrary, are a beautifully designed vehicle for engaging that world.

Even some of Nabokov's admirers, enamored of the games, have been inclined to downplay their purposefulness in illuminating the realm of experience we more or less share when we are not reading fiction. An enthusiastic essay written in 1979 by Mark Lilly vividly illustrates this predisposition. Between the two time-worn functions traditionally assigned to literature, to delight and to instruct, Lilly sees Nabokov coming down entirely on the side of delight: "His novels actually become games in which the readers are players, their task being to 'solve' the problems set by the games [of the] master-novelist. It is in this sense that we can properly refer to Nabokov as *homo ludens,* man the player."[1]

This characterization surely has considerable validity, but I think it fails to tell the whole story about Nabokov. Lilly ends up justifying Nabokov's achievement by saying that his pervasive playfulness is especially welcome in our age of "heavy seriousness." It seems to me that this needs to be put differently: the playfulness is finally about serious things—about the wrenching turns of modern history, about love and the shattering disappointments to which the lover may be vulnerable, about the terrible toll exacted through manipulative relationships, about loyalty and betrayal. As dismissive as Nabokov chose to be of reality in his pronouncements about it, the games of his fiction repeatedly lead us to experience the various emotional, moral, and even political aspects of the real world.

As an initial take on this large question, which will be addressed from different angles in the pages that follow, I would like to consider "That in Aleppo Once . . . ," a story written in English in 1943, three years after Nabokov's arrival in the United States. The narrator is a Russian émigré poet struggling to obtain the visa that will enable him to flee France after the Nazi invasion and get to the United States. He addresses his story to a certain V., a fellow Russian who has succeeded in entering the United States. V. is a writer, evidently a successful one, who is being asked to turn the narrator's story into a published text. He shares a first initial with Vladimir Nabokov, but as elsewhere in VN's fiction—one thinks of the narrator in *Pnin*, who has certain biographical features in common with Nabokov but is otherwise his antithesis—the connection is a tease: later in the story we are told that V. is the father of twins, a marker of his difference as a fictional character from his author. The presence of V. is thus a kind of game that reminds us of the ambiguous border between reality and fiction. Writers long before Nabokov have played this kind of game. At the very inception of the novel as a dominant genre in the modern era, Cervantes undertakes an elaborate maneuver of representing his book as a translation of a work by an Arab "historian" that he has discovered.

The story's title, "That in Aleppo Once," is of course taken from Othello's last speech, just before he commits suicide. At the very end, the narrator pleads with V. not to use these words as a title: "It may all end in *Aleppo* if I am not careful. Spare me, V. . . . you would load your dice with an unbearable implication if you took that for your title."[2] This ending leaves it an open question whether the narrator, in fact, is about to commit suicide. As is almost always the case in fictions constructed on a central allusion to a previous literary text, there are both parallels to and marked differences from the work invoked. The narrator, like Othello, is considerably older than his beautiful young wife, whom he adores. Unlike Desdemona, she actually betrays him, or at least claims to have done so: she is an extravagant liar, even inventing a beloved dog left behind on the couple's flight from Paris and later telling an older woman friend that her husband killed the dog, when they never had any pet. The young wife, then, is her own Iago, perhaps inventing— simply in order to torment her husband—this "brute of a man," a seller of hair lotions, with whom she spent several nights after she and her husband were temporarily separated, or perhaps actually indulging in some rough sex with the uncouth stranger.

Although it is perfectly natural for a writer as steeped in literature as Nabokov to build his fiction on a literary allusion, the procedure has been adopted by many novelists and is hardly an indication that the focus on literature somehow carries the writer away from the world of experience outside literature. Fielding makes the Joseph story in Genesis central to *Joseph Andrews*; Joyce famously organizes the episodes of *Ulysses* as parallels to episodes in the *Odyssey*; Faulkner uses the biblical story of Absalom's rebellion as a prism through which to see the catastrophic history of the American South. Yet the framework of allusion in no way detracts from the aim of each of these novels to provide a compelling representation of a particular time and place in all its ramified network of social relations and historical contexts. Some might regard the deployment of allusion as an instance of Nabokov's fondness for "codes," but as I am suggesting, it is a characteristic move not only among novelists but in literature as such. The key to the sexual betrayal plot via *Othello* is probably in the tragic hero's words in his last speech that he is "one who has loved not wisely but too well," which is a perfect characterization of the hapless émigré of the story but scarcely a piece of arcane cryptography.

In any case, I suspect that the ultimate breaking point for those who think that Nabokov in certain ways illuminates the real world and those who think he is confined to a literary playground is the response of each group of readers to style in his fiction. For the first group, his style is inventive, amusing, arresting, and at peak moments altogether sublime. For the second group, it is self-regarding, precious, annoying, and anything but a vehicle for engaging us in something like the real world. I shall have more to say about Nabokov's style in the pages that follow, but it may be instructive to look briefly into the operation of style within the restrictive compass of "That in Aleppo Once . . ." A sentence in the second paragraph of the story is a characteristic gesture that is likely to invite a polarized response.

The narrator, having briefly recalled the time when he and V. started out as poets in Russia, both continuing to write in their mother tongue after emigration, goes on to say: "And the sonorous souls of Russian verbs lend a meaning to the wild gesticulation of the trees or to some discarded newspaper sliding and pausing and shuffling again, with abortive flaps and apterous jerks along an endless windswept embankment" (p. 556). The interaction between language and things that is signaled at the beginning of the sentence is a small clue to Nabokov's view of the world. "Reality"—here those scare quotes he insists on for this term seem appropriate—is not a free-standing entity but is constituted by the words with which we represent it, the words we inevitably live with and with which we build the world around us. A small riot of personification imbues the represented scene here with life: the trees do not formulaically shake or sway in the wind but wildly gesticulate, as the windswept newspaper slides and pauses and shuffles and flaps. The one word here that will give some readers pause and drive others to their dictionaries is "apterous." The *Random House Dictionary* defines it in the following fashion: "wingless, as with some insects." One detects a signature of Nabokov the lepidopterist. It might be objected that it is unreasonable for a writer to introduce a term that few of his readers will know. I don't think such language occurs as often as is thought in Nabokov, but its use here is precisely to the point of his general conception of style: he constantly reaches for the most precise word—for shapes, for colors, for smells, and for much else—and his use of a term of entomological taxonomy (rather than merely "wingless") is the means for giving the metaphor of the wind-driven pieces of newspaper as insects a kind of scientific precision. This is not a moment of great significance in the story just now unfolding, but it is a token of how the defamiliarizing figurative language he uses concretely imparts a striking presence to all sorts of things in the world with which we are acquainted but scarcely notice. In the celebrated characterization of Viktor Shklovsky, one of the leading Russian Formalists, whose heyday coincided with the beginning of Nabokov's career, it exhibits literature's special gift for rescuing the stoniness of the stone from the dullness of automated response. This sort of exuberance of metaphoric inventiveness is often visible in Nabokov's prose, and his delight in exercising it is surely a chief reason for his otherwise slightly surprising enthusiasm for Dickens.

Yet at least as frequently it is a strategic selectiveness, the deployment of a single telling detail, that makes his writing speak to the reality of experience. In this, he may be following Flaubert, the pioneer of the art-novel—one recalls Charles Bovary's mental summary of his first marriage to a considerably older woman, whose "feet in bed were like blocks of ice." The narrator of "That in Aleppo Once . . ." does not offer any detailed description of the young woman he has married, but the following efficient notation perfectly suffices to convey both his adoration of her and his troubled relationship with her: "When I want to imagine her, I have to cling mentally to the tiny brown birthmark on her downy forearm, as one concentrates upon a punctuation mark in an illegible sentence" (p. 557). The focus on the small birthmark and the downy forearm beautifully expresses the desiring lover's enduring attachment to this pretty young woman as well as the sensuality of her presence in his imagination, while the compact simile of the punctuation mark in an illegible sentence makes it painfully clear that she remains an enigma for him. The minute physical detail, moreover, poignantly suggests that he is desperately grasping a fragment of the woman who, like Albertine in Proust, is irretrievably *disparue*, vanished, from his life. This brief sentence is a powerful demonstration of how finely wrought prose can, with the greatest concision, convey the full emotional burden of a character's experience.

Allow me to offer another brief sentence, one in which a mere parenthesis enclosing a small series of objects says all that needs to be said about the protagonist's suffering. The couple have been fleeing by train to Nice in hope of obtaining the necessary visa there and boarding a ship for America. At an intermediate stop, the narrator gets off the train in order to purchase some food. Then disaster strikes: "When a couple of minutes later I came back, the train was gone, and the muddled old man responsible for the atrocious void that faced me (coal dust glittering in the heat between naked indifferent rails, and a lone piece of orange peel) brutally told me that, anyway, I had no right to get out" (p. 559). This is a moment when Nabokov can be seen as very much in the tradition of realist fiction, much as he might have objected to the affiliation. There are no elaborate figurative maneuvers here, no real verbal pyrotechnics, but the coal dust glittering in the sun, those empty rails, wonderfully characterized as "naked indifferent," coupled with the discarded remnant of a piece of fruit (the antithesis of the edible stuff he was buying for his wife and himself) hauntingly concretize his terrible desolation. His sense of desperation is compounded by "the muddled old man," presumably the food vendor, who appears to have fatally delayed the transaction, telling him that he has no right to leave the country. There are no codes or games here and no signs of self-reflexive fiction, but terrible anguish is expressed. It is a small demonstration of the depth of emotion that is often present in Nabokov's writing, decried as it is by some as coy and cerebral. Two more extended passages from the story should suffice to show its poignant experiential burden.

The separated couple find each other again in Nice, where she tells him about that "brute of a man" to whom she offered herself, and then the two plunge into the bureaucratic labyrinth from which they may or may not extract visas for America. Here is the evocation of that labyrinth:

> So nothing remained but to torture each other, to wait for hours on end in the Prefecture, filling forms, conferring with friends who had already probed the innermost viscera of all visas, pleading with secretaries, and filling forms again, with the result that her lusty and versatile traveling salesman

became blended in a ghastly mix-up with rat-whiskered snarling officials, rotting bundles of obsolete records, the reek of violet ink, bribes slipped under gangrenous blotting paper, fat flies tickling moist necks with their rapid cold padded feet, new-laid concave photographs of your six subhuman doubles, the tragic eyes and patient politeness of petitioners born in Slutzk, Staridub, or Bobruisk, the funnels and pulleys of the Holy Inquisition, the awful smile of the bald man with the glasses, who had been told that his passport could not be found. (p. 561)

Nabokov himself did not undergo this sort of ordeal in extricating himself from France, and he actually departed by ship with his wife and child from Le Havre, not from Nice. His imagining, however, of the plight of the refugees in the Mediterranean city, including even an oblique indication of the heat in the South during this dire September, is utterly convincing. The wit of the writing is not self-serving but a vehicle for transmitting the anguish of these human figures. Thus, the desperate inspection of old, perhaps expired, visas is a probing of their innermost viscera, like pathologists conducting an autopsy in what may be a doomed effort to uncover the cause of death. The narrator's consciousness of the sexual betrayal by his wife gets all mixed up, as he confesses, with this bureaucratic nightmare. The wife's lover is not only "lusty" but "versatile," a thoroughly Nabokovian turn of wit that suggests that he is, in the poor cuckold's imagination, a man given to athletic sexual variety. The catalog of *fonctionnaires* and their implements at the prefecture, "rat-whiskered snarling officials, rotting bundles of obsolete documents, bribes slipped under gangrenous blotting paper," is devastating, some of it reminiscent of the account of decaying Chancery documents in Dickens's *Bleak House*. The "gangrenous blotting paper" is still another piece of pointed Nabokovian wit, the repulsive green of the blotting paper represented through an image of disease that reflects the narrator's pervasive sensation of disgust with this place. Another expression of disgust with these sordidly oppressive offices is the fat flies settling on necks sweating in the heat. The photos with "subhuman doubles" are of course passport photos of the protagonist: most of us turn out very badly in such photos, but the narrator in the midst of his ordeal sees himself hyperbolically as "subhuman." The photographs are concave because they are wet from just having been developed and, in the photographic technology of the day, are curling upward. The torture instruments of the Inquisition appear here because the protagonist, in the grip of this hellish bureaucracy, feels that an apparatus of power is diabolically tormenting him. The bald bespectacled man at the end of the passage is an apt concluding touch: his helplessness after the loss of the passport is palpable, and it is a strong indication of how the narrator's desperation, in the fear of being caught in an occupied country that has become a death trap, is shared by a host of others. In sum, every detail is telling, strategically chosen, and strikingly formulated, communicating a memorable sense of the fear and despair of the émigré community—all the stated places of origin are Russian—in this dark time. Nabokov the realist is on full display.

For my final example, I would like to offer a more modestly executed but nevertheless equally poignant moment. The narrator has at last obtained visas and has come with his wife to Marseille, where they are about to begin the voyage, so he imagines, to America. Armed with the tickets for the ship, he mounts the stairs (of course there is no elevator) to their hotel room. When he opens the door, this is what he finds:

I saw a rose in a glass on a table—the sugar pink of its obvious beauty, the parasitic air bubbles clinging to its stem. Her two spare dresses were gone, her comb was gone, her checkered coat was gone, and so was the mauve hairband with a mauve bow that had been her hat. There was no note pinned to the pillow, nothing at all in the room to enlighten me, for of course the rose was merely what French rhymesters call *une cheville.* (p. 562)

There are no elaborate stylistic maneuvers in the prose, and the closest the passage comes to figuration is the "parasitic" clinging of the air bubbles to the stem of the rose. Everything is enacted through the writer's shrewd choice of concrete details. The empty wardrobe speaks for itself, while the fact that the young woman has only two spare dresses reflects the poverty she shares with her distraught husband. The choice of "mauve" for the bluish purple of the hairband and bow is in keeping with the keenly visual Nabokov's general commitment to use precisely nuanced terms for colors—it is integral, he asserted more than once, to seeing the world in all its rich particularity. The wife's adopting a hairband and bow in lieu of a hat in an era when proper women wore hats—sometimes extravagant ones—whenever they dressed up might be another reflection of her poverty, or perhaps a small sartorial indication of her unfettered ways. Finally, there is that French term at the end. Like "apterous" at the beginning of the story, it is likely to annoy some readers, who may conceive it as a token of Nabokov's cultural elitism, for, after all, few will know what it means. Let me propose that the unfamiliar term serves both a mimetic and a thematic purpose. What it means in French is a hackneyed word or phrase plugged into a poem simply in order to make a rhyme (like "eyes" and "skies" in English). The narrator, we should remember, is a poet, and he surely has been immersed in French poetry and its terminology, probably since his early years in Russia and obviously after living in France after emigration. It is thus quite plausible that a person with this sort of background would invoke such a term, and not necessarily as an affectation. But the term also suggests the tricky ground that his story is treading between literary cliché and believable experience, which tends to be true of much fiction, as Nabokov is keenly aware, here and throughout his writing. The rose in water, soon to fade, is the only detail in the scene that is not an absence—that brief catalog of the wife's scant belongings which have now vanished. It shows the reader a rather paltry, sad image of beauty in the bleak hotel room and of beauty's transience, and as the single present detail in a roomful of absences it makes the scene sadly real. Yet it also looks suspiciously like a cliché, and the poet-narrator is quite aware of this, putting it down as *une cheville,* even if it was actually there at the site of his abandonment.

It may be objected that this brief story is by no means typical of Nabokov. It contains no extended passages of bravura writing; there is no flaunting of the literary artifice of the fiction, no signature butterflies, no teasing hints of the author's presence within the fiction (apart from the minimal indication that the addressee of the story shares an initial with him); and, except for the single allusion to *Othello,* there is no elaborate allusive network of the sort we will be following in several of the major novels. Yet I think "That in Aleppo Once . . ." is instructive in regard to an underlying impulse in Nabokov's writing. Although he repeatedly shows himself conscious of the multiple ways in which fiction constitutes worlds through sheer invention, deploying the technical procedures, the images, the narrative situations of antecedent literature, and though he very often delights in playing with the necessary artifice of fiction, he remains, as this story should indicate, deeply concerned with representing humanity in the toils of emotional experience and moral dilemmas, struggling with relationships, constricted by the harsh vise of historical circumstance. He is in this way more deeply anchored in the great tradition of the novel than is often thought. The flaunted artifice of his novels, the codes and complicated games he deploys in them, are not an impediment to this representational enterprise but among the principal means through which he realizes it, in concert with the fine attention to place and concrete detail that we have seen in this story. Through the chapters that follow, I shall try to show how self-reflexivity and realism work together in some of his major works.

2

Not Reading the Papers

This essay, in a much shorter form and with a somewhat different emphasis, was initially written in 1990, after I had gone to Russia during the last year of the Soviet Union for a conference on Nabokov, who until recently had been a banned writer there. It was also when the first of Brian Boyd's major two-volume biography of Nabokov had just appeared, throwing much new light on the writer. Consequently, the essay bears the stamp of the time of its composition more than any of the other pieces in this book. Nevertheless, it also extends the argument I have put forth throughout that Nabokov, for all his disdain for those caught up in the circumstantial trivia of daily life and swimming in political currents, was acutely concerned with how the political realm shapes societies and with how it affects the inner life of people living in societies. In this way, it adds a perspective to the general argument of this book.

I

Toward the end of July 1934 Vladimir Nabokov wrote from Berlin, where he had been living for twelve years, to the eminent émigré poet and critic Vladislav Khodasevich, and made one of those unqualified statements in defense of art as private expression that seem to confirm him as an incorrigible aesthete and escapist. From the city that had recently become the capital of the Third Reich, to which he had been displaced from his native Petersburg by the Bolshevik Revolution, Nabokov could tell his friend that writers should "occupy themselves only with their own meaningless, innocent, intoxicating business." In all talk about "the modern era," "*inquiétude*," and "religious renaissance," in every statement that contained the word "postwar," he sensed "the same herd instinct, the 'all-together-now' of, say, yesterday's or last century's enthusiasm for world's fairs." "I am writing my novel. I do not read the papers."[1]

All this sounds like a categorical rejection of the political realm, but it is really a refusal to contemplate the political realm on the level of fashionable formulas, with the limited language and the stunted imaginative reach of the daily press. In fact, the novel that Nabokov was working on as he wrote Khodasevich was *Invitation to a Beheading*, which conjures up an eerily revelatory fantasy world of totalitarianism. In the unlikely vehicle of a nightmarish farce, the book brings together the principles of pervasive state terror shared by Hitler and Stalin. Nabokov is an exemplary writer of his century precisely because his best work challenges easy oppositions between the aesthetic and the moral realms. He resembles the two modernists he most admired, Proust and Joyce, in attributing supreme importance to aesthetic values, but he is more like Proust in assuming that moral issues are subtly implicated in art; and for all his dedication to art, he did not have the kind of relentless self-absorption that led Joyce toward the end of his life to worry about the outbreak of a new world war only as a threat to the publication of *Finnegans Wake*. In his own experience, Nabokov had seen too painfully the terrible consequences for civilized existence of political events.

With the publication in 1990 of the first volume, *The Russian Years,* of Brian Boyd's two-volume biography, it became possible to get a much clearer picture of Nabokov's relation to Russian political and cultural history, and to the various currents of the European Russian emigration. (Boyd's achievement would continue with a second volume on Nabokov's American years.) The clarity of the picture is especially needed because a good deal of fuzziness of detail and skewed perspective was introduced into the public domain by Andrew Field, Nabokov's first biographer. In his waning years, Nabokov imprudently agreed to let Field do an "authorized" biography. The result, published in 1977 (and recycled with elaborations in 1986), was mannered, coy, factually sloppy, sometimes more about Field than about Nabokov, and showed an edge of hostility that had emerged as the biographer and his subject quarreled over formulations of the draft version.

Boyd, by contrast, a literary scholar from New Zealand and the author of a brilliant critical study of Nabokov's *Ada* who would go on to do much distinguished criticism, had done a formidable amount of patient spadework. He thoroughly examined the Nabokov collections at the Library of Congress and in Montreux, together with other pertinent archives. He scrutinized the letters and journals of everyone who came in contact with Nabokov, conducting extensive interviews with Nabokov's widow, and traveled from country to country to talk with Nabokov's sundry friends and relations.

The product of these labors is a very valuable book, though it is a little peculiar as biography. Strictly respecting Nabokov's absolute dismissal of psychological determinism, Boyd offers a chastely apsychological portrait of the writer that substitutes for psychological conjecture a kind of thematic interpretation of character. A fine critic, he chafes under the onus of biographical

narration, and from the moment that Nabokov becomes a professional writer in the early 1920s, almost half of every chapter is
devoted to a synopsis and a critical discussion of his stories,
poems, plays, and novels. Symptomatically, at the midpoint of
this first volume, the narrative is entirely set aside for twenty-
nine pages devoted to an admirable chapter-long essay, "Nabokov the Writer," with examples largely drawn from the American
novels, not the Russian ones. In all of this, Boyd offers fine
insights into *The Defense, Invitation to a Beheading, The Gift*, and
to Nabokov's general enterprise as a writer, but the momentum
of biographical report is repeatedly interrupted in a way that at
times can be a bit frustrating. This project would, after the com-
pletion of the second volume, turn out to be an impressive
thousand-page critical essay on Nabokov, rich in information
about his life and its sundry contexts, but its central, human
figure may sometimes seem a little remote.

In one respect, however, the disproportion of Boyd's biography is justified. As he abundantly shows, Nabokov—whatever
energies he devoted to his roles as son, father, husband, lover,
and maneuverer among émigré social groups—was above all,
in Stendhal's phrase, a "writing animal." The sheer quantity and
variety of his literary output, through constant economic hard-
ship, traumatic bereavement, romantic involvement, and occasional bouts of debilitating illness, are astounding. By the
time he came to the United States in 1940 at the age of forty-one
(where Boyd's first volume breaks off), he had written in Russian nine novels, two volumes of stories, four collections of
verse, several plays, not to speak of a novel composed in English
in 1938–39, *The Real Life of Sebastian Knight*, which was published a year after his arrival in America. Stylistic fireworks,
intricacies of formal design, cunningly encrypted games of
allusion, anagrams, and motifs are the hallmarks of Nabokov's

fiction, but the chief power of Boyd's reading is his argument, first taken up in his book on *Ada,* that all this play with form and surface has carefully meditated metaphysical implications. Perhaps a little surprisingly, "reality" proves to be the essential term in this persuasive conception of Nabokov's imaginative undertaking. It is a term, as Nabokov himself observed more than once, that can scarcely be used without the protective cover of quotation marks. A good many readers, put off by his archness and by the mandarin touches of his prose, have assumed that Nabokov had no interest in reality, contenting himself with the admiration of his own artifice. Boyd, on the contrary, argues for an essential connection between the meticulous empiricism of Nabokov's activity as an entomologist and his concerns as a writer: "Nabokov accepted the world as real, so real that there is always more and more to know—about the scales of a butterfly wing, about a line of Pushkin."[2]

"Always more" is the key to Nabokov's world. He assumes that the fulfillment of consciousness is in the knowledge of reality, a difficult but deeply gratifying activity. The data of experience are elusive, challenging, sometimes baffling in their stubborn, exquisite individuality. To take in the precise pale pattern of a butterfly's wing or a sunset, the delicate shading of a beautiful woman's eyelids, the venation of a side of beef hanging in a butcher's stall, the mental gymnastics of a murderer, is to overcome an inertia that allows us generally to slip through the world without really experiencing it. In Boyd's happy phrase, this is Nabokov's "secret recipe for happiness: detach the mind from accepting a humdrum succession of moments, and everything becomes magical." There is a curious and instructive correspondence, as I noted in the previous chapter, between this view and the rationale for "defamiliarization" that was articulated at just the same time, in the 1920s, by the

Russian Formalists in the Soviet Union. Although there is no indication that Nabokov read the Formalists, Viktor Shklovsky's famous declaration on the escape from automatic perception through art could be a motto for Nabokov's writing: "Art exists that one may recover the sensation of life; it exists to make one feel things, to make the stone stony."[3] One could construe both Nabokov and the Russian Formalists as parallel responses to a very modern sense of the decay of experience—a process of cultural devolution vividly described in this same period from another angle by Walter Benjamin. But there are also significant differences. The Formalists emphasized experience as potent sensation. Nabokov saw sensation and pellucid knowledge as an indissoluble fusion. The Formalists envisaged discrete objects of experience that could be felt with renewed immediacy through constantly innovative artistic means. Nabokov assumed, as Boyd implies, that reality was a kind of infinite regress of related but unique entities—snowflakes and souls—endlessly and unpredictably linked with each other through hidden patterns, layer after layer or level after level of "reality" dimly glimmering behind the one we strive to see. That is why the finely discriminated details in his fiction are repeatedly set in a barely visible web of larger connective designs.

Finally, beneath all the ingenuity in Nabokov, there is the most poignant sense of a loss—dictated, surely, by his irrevocable exile in 1917 from the cherished world of his childhood—a loss that the act of literary creation seeks to restore. Thus, the narrator of a story written in 1925, "A Guide to Berlin," proposes that the aim of literary art is "to portray ordinary objects as they will be reflected in the kindly mirrors of future times; to find in the objects around us the fragrant tenderness that only posterity will discern in the far-off times when every trifle of our plain, everyday life will become exquisite and festive in its own right"

(*The Stories of Vladimir Nabokov,* p. 157). This set of assumptions leads to a deployment of style and narrative point of view that repeatedly trips the reader off the beaten path of conventional response—through the surprise of an athletic metaphor, an odd choice of words, an unexpected angle of vision, the sheer microscopic precision of a visual perception, a bizarre conjunction of subject and tone.

Consider a modest but characteristic illustration from one of the early Russian novels, *King, Queen, Knave* (1928). Martha Dreyer is sitting in a train compartment headed for Berlin with a callow young man named Franz, whom she will make her lover, and with her husband, whose death she will eventually plot. Irritated by her husband's presence, she closes her eyes and leans back in her seat: "The sun penetrated her eyelids with solid scarlet, across which luminous stripes moved in succession (the ghostly negative of the passing forest), and a replica of her husband's cheerful face, as if slowly rotating toward her, got mixed up in this barred redness, and she opened her eyes with a start."[4] This is the sort of minute perceptual phenomenon that few novelists would take the trouble to discriminate, certainly with such precision. The mimetic success of the moment is chiefly a matter of careful observation, abetted by the happy metaphor of the photographic negative—sunlight turned scarlet under closed lids, interrupted by the vertical shapes of the passing trees, so that the intervals of light among them become red bars on the retina. (The focus on a liminal state between waking and sleep may have been encouraged by the model of Nabokov's great Russian predecessor Andrey Biely.) The rotating face of the husband among the bars might be an intimation that the presomnolent image is associated with Martha's sense of imprisonment in her sterile marriage, though Nabokov is always scrupulous about avoiding symbolic insistences. The entire moment of Martha's dozing off on the train, moreover, is an allusion, or a kind of homage, to a much grander novel about adultery—an invocation of the brilliantly realized scene early in *Anna Karenina* in which Anna, reading an English novel in her train compartment on the way to Moscow, drifts off into a dream of a more exciting life. The allusion to Tolstoy reflects Nabokov's constant awareness that all representations of reality in fiction take place against a large and complex background of established representational techniques and specific memorable instances of representation. The abiding challenge to the writer is to use them, refine them, go beyond them. As a lepidopterist, he was proud of having devised a new method of classification that involved counting the scales on butterfly wings, and his procedure as a novelist was often motivated by a similar impulse to catch what to the "communal eye" (a phrase he uses scornfully in *Pale Fire*) lay below the threshold of perception, like those luminous stripes beneath the dozing Martha's eyelids. What is below the threshold may be pure sensory experience—Nabokov's interest in such phenomena may explain his excessive admiration for the elegant, arid novels of Alain Robbe-Grillet—or it may involve something as complicated as the psychology of a deviant or an outsider, a pervert and an obsessive who is both a radiant artist and a perverter of art (Humbert Humbert); a myopic, hopelessly inept, absentminded professor who is also a bumbling moral hero (Pnin).

These considerations may help us understand what is involved in the vehemence of Nabokov's rejection, in his letter to Khodasevich, of all the ways of talking and seeing that he associates with the "herd instinct." But was he more than an elitist turning his back on the great and terrible events of his time, the unreconstructed "aristocrat" imagined by his detractors? The degree to which those events impinged on him from the age of eighteen to forty-one must be stressed. Through Lenin's seizure of power, Nabokov lost his patrimony, literally and figuratively, and was banished forever from his native ground. In 1922, at an émigré political meeting in Berlin, his father, a widely admired leader of the liberal-centrist Constitutional Democrats, was murdered by a right-wing extremist. From 1933 to 1937, he lived in Berlin under Hitler, a predicament he would have found hateful in any case but one that was particularly ominous because his wife was a Jew. (Three years later he left occupied France for America with the help of HIAS, a Jewish relief organization.) At this same time in the 1930s, Leninist state terror had swelled into Stalinist planned starvation and mass murder, counting among its victims people Nabokov had known; and his brother Sergei was arrested by the Nazis as a homosexual and was destined to perish in a concentration camp.

Against this grim background, it should be noted (and Boyd, following a hint from the émigré critic Gleb Struve, does note) that Nabokov, especially in the 1930s, devotes a good deal of his writing to political topics, for all his aestheticism. In addition to *Invitation to a Beheading,* he dealt with the menace of totalitarianism in stories like "Cloud, Castle, Lake" and "Tyrants Destroyed," and in his play, *The Waltz Invention.* Moreover, as Boyd observes, the biography-within-a-novel of the nineteenth-century socialist thinker Nikolai Chernyshevsky in *The Gift* is essentially an assault on the foundations of Marxism, a scathing criticism of the outlook that made art a stupid instrument of "progressive" ideology. The first novel that Nabokov wrote after settling in America, *Bend Sinister* (1947), is, like *Invitation,* the projection into a fictional world of the principles of the totalitarian state. Even later, as he moved on to other concerns, nightmare images of political terror still flitted through his work: the Jewish woman Pnin once loved who dies a hideous death in a concentration camp, the murderous goon Gradus in *Pale Fire*, who is sent by the revolutionary regime of Zembla to assassinate its exiled king.

Still, the essential way in which Nabokov's fiction is a serious response to twentieth-century politics is not in these intermittent confrontations with explicitly political questions, but in an underlying assumption about the relation of consciousness to reality. He perceived early on that the supreme imperative of totalitarianism was to impose a ruthless conformism on consciousness, to make human beings mechanically manipulable by reducing individual consciousness to a set of collective automatisms. The instruments of reduction were not only terror and demagoguery but also propaganda masquerading as art. He was sensitive, too, to conformist pressures in the intellectual and consumerist fashions of the democratic states—the "all-together-now" impulse that drove people to world fairs and best-selling formula-fiction—though these were diluted and merely irritating analogues to the obliteration of individual imagination that was an inner necessity of totalitarianism. Art, for Nabokov, was neither a luxury nor an escape. It was the last line of freedom's defense, the most powerful and concrete demonstration that the mind was unfettered, that there was "always more" of reality than the official repressive versions made out. "We are visitors and investigators in a strange universe, indeed," observes the narrator of *Ada*. Nabokov's fiction is devised as a sustained campaign of resistance against all who try to displace the strangeness with a flat, coercively prescribed plan of reality.

Consider an example that is both a programmatic statement of this principle and an illustration of its enactment in novelistic technique. At the end of the fourth chapter of *Bend Sinister*, Adam Krug, the philosopher protagonist, aching over the recent death of his wife, Olga, and worried by the menace of the totalitarian Russo-Germanic regime under which he lives, makes his way past an embracing adolescent couple blocking the doorway to his apartment house. They separate, the girl dashes up the stairs ahead of Krug, trailing her gaudily spangled wrap "with all its constellations—Cepheus and Cassiopeia in their eternal bliss, and the dazzling tear of Capella, and Polaris the snowflake on the grizzly fur of the Cub, and the swooning galaxies."[5]

This wild flight of association leads the philosopher Krug to reflect on Blaise Pascal's famous statement about being frightened by the starry spaces: "Those mirrors of infinite space *qui m'éffrayent*, Blaise, as they did you, and where Olga is not, but where mythology stretches strong circus nets, lest thought, in its ill-fitting tights, should break its old neck instead of rebounding with a hep and a hop"—and on the metaphor goes, for another dozen lines, showing thought the acrobat pirouetting in the "urine-soaked dust" of a circus ring as it completes its breathtaking stunt. Characteristically, the narrative procedure is not interior monologue, but the poised report of an artful narrator who selectively enters into the protagonist's point of view. The mental leap from the anonymous girl's spangled wrap to the swooning galaxies is certainly Krug's, but it is unclear whether the elaborate metaphor of thought as a tightrope walker over the abyss of infinity is supposed to occur to Krug or is, more probably, the narrator's own poetic observation on how the mind works. The key to the passage and to the novel, the very trait that confused and annoyed American reviewers when the book first appeared in 1947, is the sudden, extravagant efflorescence of the unanticipated. One hardly expects starry constellations and high-wire acts on the darkened landing of a European apartment building in a city gripped by state terror.

There is something irrepressibly celebratory about Nabokov's writing—I borrow that word from *The Art of Celebration*, an illuminating study of modernism by Alfred Appel Jr.—that manifests itself even in his bleakest works, like *Bend Sinister*. He is continually grateful, as Boyd's biography stresses, for the bounties of experience and for the mind's ability to take them in. One may argue that not everything in *Bend Sinister* fits together as tightly as all the seemingly bizarre details in *Invitation to a Beheading*, but the underlying criticism of totalitarianism in the two novels is similar. In the crucial instance of the exceptional individual, the mind itself refuses to be caged. Its athleticism, enabling it to leap from realm to realm, to turn the world into a kaleidoscope of swarming possibilities, presents a stubborn, mocking challenge to the crude, monochromatic operation of a mind without imagination, manacled by totalitarianism. So it is appropriate that this novel should include a long meditation on Shakespeare, "a man who had only to breathe on any particle of his stupendous vocabulary to have that particle live and breathe and throw out tremulous tentacles until it became a complex image with a pulsing brain and correlated limbs" (p. 107). Nabokov's devotion to the exhilarating freedom of consciousness that allows it to scale heights, skirt abysses, and peer into peculiar nooks and crannies is evident not only on every page of *Bend Sinister* but throughout his writing. *The Defense, The Gift, Lolita, Pale Fire,* and *Speak, Memory* are as much acts of resistance against the oppressive force of modern ideologies as are his two explicitly political novels.

II

The growing interest in Nabokov within the Soviet Union as communism crumbled throws a retrospective light on the political dimension of this writer who for the most part eschewed politics while adhering to his father's staunch liberal outlook. As recently as 1987, Nabokov was still a forbidden writer in the Soviet Union, read only clandestinely. His identity as an émigré, an aristocrat, and a frank anti-Communist sufficed to make him taboo in the 1920s and 1930s. Later, after his switch from Russian to English, the conspicuous international success of *Lolita* also confirmed him in the prudish eyes of the Soviet regime as a scandalously indecent writer. But in the late spring of 1990, the journal *Inostrannaia Literatura* (Foreign Literature)—an organization, like all Soviet journals, with official standing, though evidently one that kept a healthy distance from the Party-linked Writers' Union—sponsored a three-day conference on Nabokov, open to the public and covered by the press. I was among the roughly twenty-five participants, who were about equally divided between Russians and people from abroad. More than half of the foreigners were American, mostly from departments of Slavic studies, though there was also one Pole, one New Zealander (Boyd), one Canadian, one East Indian, and one West German. The Russians who gave papers were men (no women) in their thirties or forties; the recovery of Nabokov in the Soviet Union seems to be an activity of relatively young people. They were too smart and too cultivated to undertake the task in a nationalistic spirit. In fact, the convener of the conference, Nikolai Anastasiev, deputy editor of *Inostrannaia Literatura*, stressed in his introductory remarks that Nabokov was one of the great modern cosmopolitan writers and should not be appropriated as uniquely Russian. Still, quite understandably, there was some feeling on the Russian side of reclaiming a major writer who wrote for two decades in Russian, who remained steeped in Russian literary traditions, and who had been withheld from readers and scholars in the Soviet Union for all these years.

The desire to recover a lost Russian writer, and even, in a certain sense, the Russia that was lost with him, was poignantly apparent in Leningrad. After the formal sessions in Moscow, our hosts, whose institutional and individual hospitality was unflagging, took us by first-class night train to Leningrad, the city, under another name, soon to be resumed, of Nabokov's childhood. People were already beginning to call it Petersburg again, and we saw that some Communist-name street signs had been torn down. We had not quite realized that we were to be led on a kind of Nabokov pilgrimage. Indeed, although most of our Russian counterparts appeared to view him with an appropriately ironic intelligence, there were also some signs of a Nabokov cult in the making.

The young man who acted as our guide seemed to have committed to memory every step of the route on which Nabokov and his brother were taken for walks by their nanny at the dawn of the twentieth century. Peering up from the courtyard behind what was once the Nabokov town house at 47 Morskaya Street, he pointed out the high window of the room where little Volodya would go to pee. The ground floor of the house is now an institutional library. After some complicated negotiation with the dour babushka who barred the entrance, our group was allowed to enter and glimpse the still-grand staircase with its splendid stained-glass windows on the first landing, and what was once the gracious wood-paneled dining room. We were also taken to the site of the Nabokov estate at Vyra, about fifty kilometers outside the city. The house so vividly evoked in *Speak, Memory* was burned to the ground by the Nazis before they fled, but the wooded landscape and the vistas of the Ore-dezh River are still ravishing. One easily understands how the eighteen-year-old Nabokov was able to carry with him into exile, not a resentment over lost goods, but a passion for the luminous beauty of nature that he constantly remembered in his writing and variously rediscovered in regions to the west.

At the turn of the century, Petersburg must have been one of the most spectacular cities in Europe. It is still quite beautiful—until you come close to the buildings and realize how deterio-rated they are, flaking, cracking, begrimed, marked with the stigmata of seven decades of neglect, like almost everything in the Soviet Union. Nabokov, although he is many other things, as the sundry conference papers stressed, is inevitably associ-ated with that moment just before the cultural splendor was abruptly eclipsed. The point is not merely that he grew up in a glittering aristocratic world, lived in that grand house on Mor-skaya Street, was transported to his liberal high school (some-what to his embarrassment) in a limousine, but that the pol-ished artifice of his writing is a monument more lasting than bronze to a vanished Russian culture. It expresses not only the refinement of Russian aesthetic traditions but also a humane liberalism that stood in opposition to the absolutism of the czars. In Russia, it seems, things now change faster than you can imagine, and nobody has a clue as to how it will all turn out, though, given Russia's history of despotic rule, optimism is not warranted. The fortunes of Nabokov are striking proof of the first of these two principles.

On our way to Russia, my wife and I met an Italian professor of philosophy at Bagni di Lucca who said he traveled frequently to the Soviet Union. When we explained the purpose of our visit, he observed that, yes, it's quite remarkable that the Rus-sians should be sponsoring a conference on Nabokov, but there would be one text about which we would hear nothing, and that was *Lolita*. At the Moscow airport we were met by a woman who was on the staff of *Inostrannaia Literatura*, and, to our surprise, we were taken to stay at her apartment. (It emerged that the journal did not have sufficient political clout to get first-class hotel rooms in Moscow, so we were all lodged graciously by members of the editorial staff or by writers.) In her living room, crowded with bookshelves, a grand piano, a double bed, a large desk, and a dining table, we discovered a newly published copy of *Lolita* in Nabokov's own Russian translation. One may assume that, like his other books, it had been produced in a large printing—perhaps one hundred thousand copies—that would be entirely snapped up soon after publication.

We grasped what a shocking transformation this represented at the end of the last Moscow session. A woman journalist had requested permission to address the group on a matter that she thought might be of interest. Speaking in emphatic, rapid-fire Russian (an American colleague improvised a translation), she explained that she had just covered a court case involving the retrial of a man sentenced only three years previous to seven years in prison on a pornography charge: he had distributed copies of *Lolita*. The court did not exonerate him, but his sentence was commuted to three-and-a-half years, so that he would be eligible for imminent release. Nobody explained the contradiction of sustaining the classification of pornography for a book that had just been legally published.

And then the recent suppression of literature through the penal system was brought still closer to home. Among the Russian participants at the conference was a Leningrader named Mikhail Meylakh, a man in his forties who started out as a scholar of Provençal poetry, and who now makes his living at least in part as the correspondent for a Paris-based émigré journal, a vocation that would have been inconceivable just a few years earlier. What had interrupted his professional career, I discovered, was his arrest in 1983 for possessing a copy of *Speak, Memory.* He was sentenced to four years in a labor camp for this crime against the state. He was not in the least inclined to be melodramatic about his experience: he did what he felt he had to do, and he was fully prepared to suffer the consequences. When I asked him how he had managed without a regular job, since he was scarcely employable after being freed from detention, he explained, quite simply, that in Communist society money was not very important. There's not much you can buy, he explained, and what there is doesn't cost very much; if you have a place to live and a few friends, you get along.

I was moved by both of these stories and referred to them at a public forum in Leningrad, at the Palace of Labor, once a palace of Alexander III, at which we were all invited to make brief personal statements about Nabokov. I recounted that the first thing I had written on Nabokov, over twenty years earlier, was an essay on *Invitation to a Beheading,* in which I tried to explain how a writer could permit himself the seeming luxury of an exploration of art and artifice in a novel dealing with totalitarianism. My answer in 1969 had been that totalitarianism, by its logic, needs to destroy real art and replace it with fake art, *poshlust,* because art is an exercise of individual consciousness that cannot be tolerated. I said that it was only now, confronted by these two stories of participants at our conference, that I realized the full human implications of the idea I had sought to express then. At a party the next night I learned that one of the panel coordinators had been on the phone for three hours in the middle of the night with an anonymous caller who was indignant about the political provocation delivered by the American professor.

Talking about Nabokov in Russia makes one acutely aware of the never-never land that American academia has become. Literature in our own academic circles is regularly dismissed, castigated as an instrument of ideologies of oppression, turned into a deconstructive plaything, preferentially segregated by the pigmentation and the sexual orientation of the writers, or entirely displaced by clinical case studies, metaphysical treatises, psychoanalytic theories, and artifacts of popular culture. Those of us who made the journey to Moscow came away with the sense that there are still people in the world for whom literature matters urgently, for whom literature has a strong and illuminating connection with the real world. When dark times require it, there are even people prepared to risk their freedom for the truth of a writer's vision. It is surely instructive that Nabokov should speak so tellingly to younger Russians in the process of attempting to extricate themselves from seven decades of systematic oppression. To the casual eye or, perhaps one should say, to the communal eye, he is a mannered, self-indulgently aesthetic writer, playing virtuoso tunes on the fiddle of private experience as the world burns. In truth, however, he is a novelist obsessed with love and loss, concerned with how a misdirected aesthetic impulse twists lives and inflicts pain, with how the public realm can violate the territory of individual existence, including the sanctum of the mind.

Brian Boyd summarizes Nabokov's character in three salient traits: his unflagging self-assurance, "his intense, almost ruthlessly concentrated feelings toward others," and "his unrelenting individualism." The second of these three traits helps to explain the passionate feeling beneath the surface glitter of his prose. He needed the self-assurance and the individualism to keep him going through decades when his writing went stubbornly against the grain of literary fashion and could scarcely sustain his material existence. He never wavered from writing the kind of books he knew he had to write, not in the face of political cataclysms during the European years, not in the face of misguided advice from American publishers and critics before his great success with *Lolita*. Shortly after finishing that novel in 1954, he described it, in a letter to James Laughlin, as a "timebomb." The same may be said after all these years of many of his books. He repeatedly demonstrated that fidelity to the imagination is a form of political courage, a recognition now shared by readers in his native land who are exercising the same rare virtue.

3

Lolita Now

After almost three-quarters of a century, how are we now to think about *Lolita*? It may well be the most commented-on novel written in English in the past hundred years, alongside Joyce's *Ulysses.* In the case of *Ulysses,* the imperative for commentary is chiefly a consequence of the invitation to exegesis generated by that novel's dense network of allusions and the multiple complexities of its structure. In fact, Alfred Appel Jr., in the introduction to his splendid *Annotated Lolita,* has observed certain affinities between *Lolita* and *Ulysses* in the centrality of parody for both novels, in their resourceful deployment of popular culture, and, of course in their shared elaborate mobilization of literary allusions. Nabokov, we should recall, was a great admirer of *Ulysses. Lolita* has its own formal intricacies, and these have been duly explicated by much apt criticism ever since its initial American publication in 1958. Yet the more obvious reason why *Lolita* has elicited so much discussion through the years is the moral questions raised by its subject. The crudest notes of the discussion were first struck by readers who imagined that the author must be a pervert and that the novel he wrote was altogether a sordid thing. In more sophisticated guise, Norman Podhoretz and some other conservative writers have contended that *Lolita* may corrupt morals and must be approached with caution by right-thinking people. Inevitably, the novel has also been excoriated on the feminist left. An influential article by Rebecca Solnit in the online journal *Literary Hub* seems to include *Lolita*—the meaning is a bit opaque in her diffuse exposition—in the category of novels that represent women as "disposable," or "dirt," or "silent, absent, or worthless" (December 27, 2015).

Serious considerations of the novel have properly dismissed all such views, and, indeed, many of the earliest critics recognized it as a literary achievement of the first order of originality (but not Nabokov's erstwhile friend Edmund Wilson, who thought it regrettable). In fact, strong arguments have been made for the moral character of the book, and these need not be repeated here. What may be at issue for readers of *Lolita* in the twenty-first century is how to regard the book in an age when our culture has become so conscious of the sexual exploitation of children and of women in general, young or otherwise. This is, of course, a social problem that is alarmingly widespread, but it must be said that the public exposure of certain especially egregious cases has led much of the public to hairtrigger responses to any activity even obliquely related to such appalling exploitation. It is a sign of our confused times that Dan Franklin, the editor-in-chief of the esteemed London publishing house Jonathan Cape, has declared that he would not publish *Lolita* if it were submitted to him now. His judgment stems either from a misguided reading of the book or, more likely, from an acute nervousness about how new readers might now respond to it. Is this awareness likely to make it altogether uncomfortable to read the first-person narrative of a middle-aged male who repeatedly, extravagantly, and at times brutally commits carnal acts with a pubescent girl who is quite helpless to free herself from him? Novelists, of course, have not infrequently chosen to write books about deviant, criminal, or murderous characters—Humbert Humbert is all three—but the sexual exploitation of a child surely touches a raw nerve, especially now. (One highly intelligent reader, recently reading *Lolita* for the first time, told me that he could see it was a brilliant novel but found it difficult to stick with because of the subject.)

I would like to suggest that the way Humbert's story is constructed anticipates this sort of discomfort, in a sense even aligning itself with the discomfort. Nabokov, devoted as he was to the supreme importance of art, had been concerned since his Russian novels with the phenomenon of the perverted artist, the person who uses a distorted version of the aesthetic shaping of reality to inflict suffering on others, and Humbert Humbert is his most extreme representation of such distortion. The perversion of the artistic impulse is a vital subject for Nabokov precisely because art matters so much to him.

The first thing that should be noted about the treatment of this subject in *Lolita* is that Humbert Humbert clearly regards himself as a monster, repeatedly emphasizing his own monstrosity. This goes along with the fact that he is insane, as he frankly admits, and that he has been several times institutionalized in asylums. Humbert's assertions of his own moral repulsiveness abound in the novel. "I am," he says of himself early in his story, as a boarder in the Haze home, "like one of those pale inflated spiders you see in old gardens. Sitting in the middle of a luminous web and giving jerks to this or that strand."[1] With Lolita tantalizingly sitting in his lap on the Haze davenport, he invokes a familiar fairy tale that here will have no happy ending as he wriggles in order "to improve the secret system of tactile correspondence between beast and beauty—between my gagged, bursting beast and the beauty of her dimpled body in its innocent cotton frock" (p. 59). It might be noted that Humbert's framing of this allusion altogether reduces the man to his imperious sexual member. Elsewhere, he recognizes "that nothing but pain and horror would result from the expected rapture." When he finally consummates his lust for Lolita, he declares that it was she who seduced him, not an altogether improbable claim given her sexual precociousness. But she for her part says, fearing he has torn her internally—though it is unclear whether she might be merely joking—that she ought to report him to the police for rape, and at least in a moral sense as well as in the statutory one, this could be quite right. The yearlong frenzy of sexual gratification with a sometimes reluctantly submissive, sometimes resistant twelve-year-old has its particularly sordid moments beyond its intrinsic sordidness, as when Humbert insists on sex when Lolita is running a high fever or in his repeated bribing her with magazines and treats to make herself available to his insatiable desire. Humbert's admission of all this repeated abuse culminates near the end of the novel in his often-cited recognition as he watches schoolchildren at play that he has deprived Lolita of her childhood. But a summarizing assessment of what he has perpetrated in the throes of his obsession occurs earlier, as he and Lolita head back east in his car:

> We had been everywhere. We had really seen nothing. And I catch myself thinking today that our long journey had only defiled with a sinuous trail of slime the lovely, truthful, dreamy, enormous country that by then, in retrospect, was no more to us than a collection of dog-eared maps, ruined tour books, old tires, and her sobs in the night—every night, every night—the moment I feigned sleep. (pp. 175–176)

Here the defiling of America and the defiling of Lolita are virtually interchangeable. This self-revelatory moment, coming at the end of a chapter, is telling in two ways: first the invocation of slime, cognate with the earlier image of the spider, to indicate the repulsiveness of this sexual odyssey, and then, at the end of the little catalog of the detritus of the journey, interwoven with it and constituting Humbert's first report of this wrenching fact—Lolita's sobbing through it all, night after night.

If *Lolita* were nothing but this, it would merely be a riveting and also unappetizing representation of a sexually obsessed madman, but what is enacted in the novel is more complicated and more interestingly ambiguous. In the afterword Nabokov wrote to *Lolita* in 1956 for the American publication of excerpts in the *Anchor Review*, he offers a curious origin for the idea of the novel. When he was laid up with illness in Paris in 1940, he came across a newspaper story about a caged ape in the Jardin des Plantes that had been given charcoal and paper and produced a sketch of the bars enclosing him. (One thinks of Rilke's famous poem about the tiger, "Au Jardin des Plantes," and the line, "It seemed to him there were a thousand bars / and behind those bars no world.") The ape inspired Nabokov to write a Russian story with a plot roughly like that of *Lolita,* but, unhappy with the piece, he destroyed it.

What does an ape in a cage drawing his prison have to do with *Lolita*? The obvious answer is that Humbert Humbert's predicament is of a man hopelessly imprisoned by his obsession. The narrative he produces is the representation of his prison, which is not an encirclement of vertical bars but rather an alluring and also vulnerable girl whom he has desperately fixed as the object of his desire. This transformation of a cage into a sexual obsession has a double effect: Lolita as its object is repeatedly celebrated in radiant prose as a thing of beauty;

and the reader is led to perceive Humbert not only with horror but with a qualified kind of sympathy as a man hideously trapped in his own impulses that inflict grave harm on someone he comes to love and that in the end destroy him. It is relevant in this connection that the Russian story Nabokov discarded ended with the suicide of its perverted protagonist. The central paradox of *Lolita*, and one of the things that makes it a great novel and not just the story of a psychopath, is that one simultaneously recoils from its narrator and is drawn into both the anguish and the lyric exuberance of his point of view.

Especially in regard to the second of these contradictory responses, the extraordinary style of the novel surely takes the book well beyond the fictional case study of a madman. Nabokov himself characterized the book as his love affair with the English language, and there are few other novels since Joyce that deploy its resources with such pyrotechnic virtuosity. In the famous first paragraph, which is a spectacular prose poem, Humbert ends by saying: "You can always count on a murderer for a fancy prose style." Humbert, with his inventor standing firmly behind him, is wonderfully having it both ways: the extravagance of the musical prose might push to the brink of excess, and Humbert is perfectly aware of this, yet the prose is glorious and is surely a part of the reader's enjoyment of this troubling story. This is the narrative of a man repeatedly doing something morally ugly conveyed in language that is often quite beautiful. The contradiction between subject and style poses a certain moral dilemma for readers, who may well relish the novel and at the same time feel uneasy about the delight they take in it. This double take is perhaps part of Nabokov's intention.

For a characteristic instance of this tricky balancing act, let us return briefly to Humbert on the davenport in the Haze home with Lolita, evidently unaware of his sexual excitement, sitting in his lap. As he approaches climax, deliberately prolonging the pleasure, he says, in a phrase that shrewdly defines his relationship with the prepubescent girl, "Lolita had been safely solipsized." He continues in his habitual extravagant style:

> The implied sun pulsated in the supplied poplars; we were fantastically and divinely alone; I watched her, rosy, gold-dusted, beyond the veil of my controlled delight, unaware of it, alien to it, and the sun was on her lips, and her lips were apparently still forming the words of the Carman-barman ditty that no longer reached my consciousness. Everything was now ready. The nerves of pleasure had been laid bare. [...] I was above the tribulations of ridicule, beyond the possibilities of retribution. In my self-made seraglio, I was a radiant and robust Turk, postponing the moment of actually enjoying the youngest and frailest of his slaves. (p. 60)

This entire scene is the most explicitly sexual moment in the novel—after this, Nabokov pointedly refrains from explicit representations of sex—but it is also something rather different. The murderer's fancy prose is exquisitely orchestrated in a virtually musical sense, the passage beginning with a spectacular set of alliterations that also incorporates a rhyme: "The implied sun pulsated in the supplied poplars." The sun is "implied" probably because Humbert, totally focused on Lolita and his pleasure, is not directly observing the sun and the "supplied" poplars on which it is shining, though he does notice the sunlight on her lips. Beyond that detail, Lolita's presence, radiant for Humbert, is evoked only in the brief phrase "rosy, gold-dusted" because Humbert is completely concentrated on his own sexual excitement. I would propose that verbal pyrotechnics of the kind one sees here, which are abundantly deployed throughout the novel, are a source of delight for readers, perhaps even eliciting a certain sense of admiration for Humbert's "sensibility" or his inventiveness, though the acts he performs trigger moral revulsion. The novel's perverted protagonist is manifestly a man of high culture—and, at the same time, following the precedent established by Joyce, avidly attentive as well to popular culture—and so this passage, like so many others in the book, spins a web of allusions in its very representation of sexual arousal. The invocation of Carmen, one of several in the novel, probably refers to Mérimée's novella rather than to the opera based on it, as Alfred Appel Jr. plausibly indicates in his note, thus conjuring up from fiction a young, sexually alluring woman, here appearing in a silly ditty. Humbert as a Turk in his seraglio, depicted in still another alliterative chain ("In my self-made seraglio, I was a radiant and robust Turk") taps into an old cliché of Western culture in which the Orient is figured as a theater of exotic sexual license. Leopold Bloom plays more than once with this same Orientalist notion. Again, I think that the articulation of Humbert's fantasy produces a double effect. A reader may enjoy the exuberance of his inventiveness, but surely what the fantasy reveals about his intentions is repugnant. What is especially telling is the phrase "enjoying the youngest and frailest of his slaves." Presumably, this compliant or helpless victim of Humbert-as-Turk's lasciviousness is almost or actually a child, and the fact that she is the "frailest" of the female slaves in the seraglio betrays his awareness of Lolita's vulnerability, an aspect of her that may well pique his twisted desire. What I have characterized as the balancing act of Nabokov's prose in this novel is abundantly evident here.

I would like to offer a final example of the odd allure created by Humbert's writing, a passage in which the sheer literariness of the writing is especially prominent. It is Humbert's first sighting of Lolita, peering at him over her dark glasses as she sunbathes on the patio. Her appearance will present to Humbert, or so he claims, the very image of Annabel Leigh, his first love met on the Riviera when both were still preteens, and then forever lost to him through an early death:

> It was the same child—the same frail, honey-hued shoulders, the same silky supple bare back, the same chestnut head of hair. A polka-dotted black kerchief tied around her chest hid from my aging ape eyes, but not from the gaze of young memory, the juvenile breasts I had fondled one immortal day. And, as if I were the fairy-tale nurse of some little princess (lost, kidnapped, discovered in gypsy rags through which her nakedness smiled at the king and his hounds), I recognized the tiny dark-brown mole on her side. With awe and delight (the king crying for joy, the trumpets blaring, the nurse drunk) I saw again her lovely indrawn abdomen where my southbound mouth had briefly paused; and those puerile hips on which I had kissed the crenulated imprint left by the hem of her shorts—that last mad immortal day behind the "Roches Roses." The twenty-five years I had lived since then, tapered to a palpitating point, and vanished. (p. 39)

The idea of a formative experience in early life imprinting itself so indelibly on the psyche that the person becomes its lifelong captive is, as quite a few commentators have noted, Nabokov's mockery of the Freudian notion of causation of sexual pathology by childhood trauma, a notion he famously despised. Given that it plays an altogether determinative role in Humbert's perversion, one must conclude that the "psychology" of the novel, based as it is on a parody of Freud, can scarcely be regarded as realistic. It is a central instance in which playfulness is paramount in this representation of a sexual deviant, an unanticipated conjunction of manner and subject that may compel us to reconsider how to think about Humbert Humbert. In one respect, he is a compelling fictional representation of a disturbed person that one can readily relate to troubling manifestations of this kind of disturbance in the real world; in another respect, he is a kind of pawn in an inventive literary game.

One should note that the caged ape in the Jardin des Plantes breaks through the surface here in Humbert's self-denigrating characterization of his own "aging ape eyes." He proceeds to embark on the fantasy of the little princess kidnapped by gypsies—the introduction of gypsies ties in with the allusions to Carmen, who is a gypsy—comically casting himself, a male figure to uncomfortable excess, as the nurse of the vanished infant. The story of the kidnapped child rediscovered in adulthood through the recognition of a birthmark is one that originates in the Greek romances of Late Antiquity and continues to lead a literary life in the Early Modern period and beyond. Fielding, for example, utilizes it in *Joseph Andrews,* birthmark and all, with the kidnappers there identified as gypsies, a European fantasy of that era. Nabokov, then, is playing not only with Freud but with the contrivance of an old tale told many times ever since the Greeks. What may properly be described as the high jinks of Humbert's consciousness, however tormented he often may be, is on display as he quickly switches roles from nurse to king, clearly the child's father, crying for joy over her discovery. The fact that the nurse is imagined to be drunk at this moment is a wildly extraneous and incongruous detail, Humbert indulging in a riot of the imagination as he re-creates for his self-explanatory purposes this old story.

In regard to his function as a narrator of the novel, it should be kept in mind that he speaks in two different, intertwined modes: his language reflects an obsessive and, indeed, deranged mind, as in the excessive, doubled insistence on "immortal" in this passage; and it also deploys the resources of Nabokov, shrewd and witty observer and master stylist. One might note here the lovely precision of the adjective in "the crenulated imprint" and the wit of "my southbound mouth" to refer to the ultimate sexual destiny toward which the mouth is traveling. The two twelve-year-olds on the Riviera, it seems, were going a step beyond ordinary preadolescent fooling around. The wonderful concluding sentence goes on to strike a distinctively Nabokovian note. It is strongly reminiscent of at least a couple of sentences in *Speak, Memory*, a book cast in its initial version not long before the composition of *Lolita*. The literary and, one could also say, stylistic recapture of the past is an urgent undertaking for Nabokov, splendidly achieved in *Speak, Memory*, and in *Lolita*, the intellectual joke of a "Freudian" childhood experience becomes also, at least at this moment, an emotionally fraught and joyous realization of the past returned in all its luminous presence.

This concert of surprising and vividly inventive effects in the passage, and elsewhere in the novel as well, leads me to propose an aspect of the readerly experience one would certainly not expect in the narrative of a sexual abuser of young girls: for all the moral dubiety of the protagonist's story, it is *fun* if also at the same time troubling to read *Lolita*, and anyone who denies this is likely to be suffering from terminal moralism or simply is not a sufficiently literary reader. In this important regard, we should now consider the essential role of parody in this novel, for this, too, is not something generally associated with the fictional portrayal of psychopaths.

Parody, of course, is pervasive in Nabokov's novels. What its presence necessarily implies is that we must see the novel not as a direct representation of reality—a word, that, according to Nabokov, as I am constrained to note again, has to always be wrapped around with scare quotes—but rather as a response to the world outside literature entirely mediated by literature, which is to say, both the novelist's own literary contrivances and the variegated background of literary tradition on which he chooses to draw. Nabokov, as criticism through the decades has abundantly shown, constantly calls attention to the status of his fiction as literary artifice, executing what the Russian Formalists of the early twentieth century referred to as "laying bare the device." The double edge, however, of this procedure as he practices it may be a little hard to get a handle on. *Invitation to a Beheading* and *Bend Sinister* are certainly ostentatiously self-reflexive novels, but they are also serious engagements with the horrors of totalitarianism, whose potential for the wholesale extirpation of humanity was all too evident during the years when they were composed. Much the same is true of the totalitarian state fantasized by Kinbote in *Pale Fire*. Nabokov's early novel *The Defense* calls attention to its own artifices, as we would expect, but it is also a wrenching representation of a genius trapped in the world of chess that is the vehicle of his genius. One could extend this catalog of grave human predicaments, historical or personal, confronted through the medium of self-reflexive fiction in all of Nabokov's novels.

In *Lolita*, then, we get the probing portrait of a sexual deviant who kidnaps a girl-child and inflicts great harm on her, conveyed through a novel that reminds us of its status as an invented fiction and constantly plays quite exuberantly with literary tradition. Parody is ubiquitous. It begins on the first page of the novel with the quotation from Poe's "Annabel Lee," a poem that lends the name Annabel Leigh to Humbert's first love. Is she, after all, a "real" character in a novel or a kind of personified citation, Humbert living out the role of the male speaker in Poe's poem? (For a fine account of the Poe resonances, readers should consult the long note on this first reference by Alfred Appel in *The Annotated Lolita*, pp. 328–332.) References to the Poe poem are scattered through the novel, with a special emphasis on angels, invoking the "winged seraphs" of "Annabel Lee." Parodies or in many cases satiric references in the novel include Mérimée, A. E. Housman, T. S. Eliot, Arthur Conan Doyle, Pierre de Ronsard, and many other writers. The elaborate development of Clare Quilty as Humbert's doppelgänger harks back to Dostoevsky's *The Double*, the work of a writer whom Nabokov despised, as well as to Poe's story "William Wilson." Parody is also deployed generically, as in the old romance story of the kidnapped child discovered through a birthmark, or in the desperate, farcical physical battle between Quilty and Humbert, about which he himself observes, "elderly readers will surely recall at this point the obligatory scene in the Westerns of their childhood." All these parodic elements have a paradoxical effect. Humbert is an appallingly twisted figure repeatedly operating in a literary landscape evoked through his own rich background in culture high and low. In the climactic scene with Quilty, we do not cease to see him as a violently jealous lover seething with rage against the man who has stolen his beloved girl from him, but the scene, with its plethora of parodic literary and cinematic references, is also hilarious, fun and horror interfused.

Nabokov approaches two things with the utmost seriousness: the profoundly consequential act of sexually exploiting a child and the instrument of art through which the moral issue is represented. For all the fun and games of the play with artifice, moving emotions are expressed, as in the great moment near the end, often observed, when Humbert discovers the now-pregnant Lolita with "her adult, rope-veined narrow hands and her goose-flesh white arms, and her shallow ears, and her unkempt armpits" (which earlier were called "pristine" when he watched her at tennis), and he can assert, "I loved her more than anything I had ever seen or imagined on earth, or hoped for anywhere else" (p. 277).

The defining dimension of art in *Lolita* must be kept in mind. Parody and the overlapping practice of allusion are essential to the fun of the novel at the same time that they point again and again to its status as a work of literature. Allusion itself is intrinsic to the dynamic of most literature: you would scarcely think of writing a story or a novel or a sonnet or an epic if you had no familiarity with such works, and allusion, through which you insert your own writing in the body of its predecessors, remaking them and often challenging them as you invoke them, is a recurrent modality for creating new literature. Parody may be thought of as a special category of allusion, usually in a comic and critical vein. These twin processes in *Lolita* constitute an implicit affirmation of the artfulness of the novel, of the pervasive operation in it of literary art. That art is of course manifested in the spectacular prose Nabokov creates for his deranged narrator, at times deliberately over the top in keeping with his derangement but very often brilliantly inventive, witty, finely lyrical, and on occasion quite moving.

Here is a moment when Humbert introduces circus performance as a metaphor for art—the same trope will recur in *Ada*—that suggests how artistic skill can convey the plight of a pathetic and unseemly character, which is precisely what his author has done for him: "We all admire the spangled acrobat with classic grace meticulously walking his tight rope in the talcum light; but how much rarer art there is in the sagging rope

expert wearing scarecrow clothes and impersonating a grotesque drunk!" (p. 249). One way, in fact, to characterize *Lolita*
is as the most troubling, and touching, representation of a morally grotesque figure in the fiction of the last century.

At the very end of his painful story, Humbert in his prison
cell, his death imminent, affirms that he has used his fleeting
time to make Lolita "live in the minds of later generations." He
then goes on to proclaim these grand concluding lines: "I am
thinking of aurochs and angels, the secret of durable pigments,
prophetic sonnets, the refuge of art. And this is the only im-
mortality you and I may share, my Lolita" (p. 309). The very last
word of the novel, as Alfred Appel has observed, is the same as
the first, affirming a kind of architectonic unity for the novel as
a whole. The reference in "aurochs" to the cave paintings of
early humans and in "angels, the secret of durable pigments" to
Renaissance art sets this narrative in a rich tradition of art going
all the way back to prehistory, much of it still enduring.

There is a certain ambiguity as to who is speaking here at the
end. Of course, it has to be Humbert, reflecting on what turns
out to be in the end the truly beloved human subject of his story
as he senses his own end approaching. Yet his voice merges with
Nabokov's in the proclamation of the perdurable power of art.
The real identification of the novelist with his protagonist is not
in regard to Humbert's perversion, as some early readers of the
book misguidedly imagined, but in the celebration of art as a
fixative of beauty and feeling, anguish and love. It is this, finally,
that lifts *Lolita* above the currents of shifting attitudes toward
sexual exploitation or toward sex itself. The novel is obviously
not a case study in perversion, as the highly parodic foreword
by the fictional psychologist John Ray Jr. would have it. It is also
something more than the compelling fictional portrait of a

repellently disturbed person. A murderer may have a fancy prose style, but the prose turns out to be both arresting and evocative, at moments sublime, leading us to experience through the moral murk of the narrator a great love story that seeks to join the company of the cave paintings of Lascaux and the sublime angels of Giotto and Raphael.

4

Nabokov's Game of Worlds

Paris is but a dream, Gabriel is but a reverie (a charming one).
Zazie the dream of a reverie (or of a nightmare) and all this
story the dream of a dream, the reverie of a reverie, scarcely
more that the typewritten delirium of an idiotic novelist (oh!
sorry).

—RAYMOND QUENEAU, *ZAZIE DANS LE MÉTRO*

In the large envelope I carried I could feel the hardcornered,
rubberbanded batches of index cards. We are absurdly
accustomed to the miracle of a few written signs being able to
contain immortal imagery, involutions of thought, new worlds
with live people, speaking, weeping, laughing.

—VLADIMIR NABOKOV, *PALE FIRE*

Vladimir Nabokov is the preeminent practitioner of what Jorge
Luis Borges, in a famous essay on *Don Quixote*, called "partial
magic" in the novel, from Cervantes' days down to our own.
This does not mean that he is necessarily the greatest of self-
conscious novelists: even his most brilliant books could hardly
be said to "surpass" *Tristram Shandy*, *Tom Jones*, or *Don Quixote*.
What it does mean is that he has been more self-conscious

about his novelistic self-consciousness than any of his predecessors or imitators, more sharply focused on a continuing critical recapitulation of a whole literary tradition. The self-consciousness of a Sterne or a Fielding is that of the pioneer of a new genre exploring its possibilities and its relation to its antecedents; the self-consciousness of Nabokov presupposes a crammed history of achievement and decline and renewal in the genre from the eighteenth century to the modern masters. Nabokov's intensified awareness, moreover, of artifice and literary history has translated itself into an oeuvre of an abundance and variety scarcely equaled among self-conscious novelists. In an age when many serious novelists, whatever their orientation, produce a scant handful of titles in a lifetime, Nabokov, beginning in 1926, published seventeen novels, nine in Russian and eight in English, to which one can add seven Russian plays, several volumes of short stories and poems in both languages, and *Speak, Memory*, one of his major imaginative achievements, cast in the form of an autobiography. The extent and variety of Nabokov's oeuvre make it particularly instructive for an understanding of the self-reflexive novel. All of his novels since the second one, *King, Queen, Knave* (1928), are in one way or another novels of flaunted artifice, but since they experiment with different strategies and since they are not all equally successful, they offer not only a whole spectrum of fictional self-consciousness but also some monitory instances of the traps, the inherent limitations, of this mode of fiction.

Nabokov's extraordinary inventiveness endows even his flawed, or slighter, works with considerable interest for the critical reader, but of his seventeen novels, I would be inclined to argue for just four as sustained masterpieces from beginning to end: *The Gift* and *Invitation to a Beheading* of the Russian novels, and still more impressive, *Lolita* and *Pale Fire* of the English ones. Perhaps one should add *Pnin*, less ambitious than these four but a jewel of a novel. Early novels such as *King, Queen, Knave*; *The Eye*; *Laughter in the Dark*; and *Despair* tend in various ways to press matters of design in a fashion that restrictively flattens the characters. The patterns of parody and obtruded artifice are cunningly devised, but the constructed fictional world, however ingenious, is hardly allowed sufficient vitality to give the dialectic between fiction and "reality" the vigorous to-and-fro energy that it requires: a play of competing ontologies cannot fully engage us when one of the competitors, the invented world of the fiction, too often seems like intellectual contrivance. Or, to cite a somewhat different but related example, *The Real Life of Sebastian Knight* (1941), Nabokov's first English novel and the one rather perversely designated by Edmund Wilson as the author's best, is an intriguing introduction to the poetics of the self-reflexive novel, but, like Unamuno's *Mist*, it is more interesting for its theory than for its realized fiction. A conundrum-novel, it gives the reader subtle pleasure in solving its puzzles of narrator and narration, subject and object, but its enticing descriptions of a "prismatic" novel and of parody as a springboard for the expression of the highest emotions would have to await *Lolita* (1955), *Pale Fire* (1962), and *Ada* (1969) for a forceful translation into fulfilled art. If the self-conscious novel tends on one side to excessive cerebralism, to an ascetic avoidance of the pungent juices of ordinary fictional life, it tends on the other side to an unchecked playfulness that may become self-indulgent.

Even a master like Joyce does not always draw the line between meaningful parody and schoolboyish verbal horseplay (one thinks of the hammering insistence on mock-heroic language in some passages of the Cyclops section, like the wedding of the trees, or the lengthy parodies of successive English styles through the ages in the Oxen of the Sun). Nabokov's character-istic indulgences are wordplay and allusions, though he has made both of these beautifully functional in his most successful fictions. Even a powerfully original book, however, may in this regard be a mixed bag. Thus, *Bend Sinister* (1947) is a brilliant companion piece to *Invitation to a Beheading* as a dystopian novel, and its central allusion to *Hamlet* has complex reverbera-tions in the major concerns of the book; but its prose, though often wonderfully strange and sumptuous, at times strikes one as overwrought, gratuitously arcane, while the allusions to Mal-larmé, Melville, and to various best sellers of the 1940s seem too much a game the author is playing with himself.

Again in *Ada*, one finds a mixture of thematically justified allusions and gratuitous ones, of richly textured expressive prose and preciosity. The allusions to Marvell, Baudelaire, Chateaubriand, and Byron are imaginatively integrated with one another, suggestively reinforcing both each other and the fictional argument, but one wonders about the references to T. S. Eliot, John Updike, and a variety of lesser writers, about the quibbles with Freud, the constant trilingual punning, the baroque quality of some of the prose. It would be ungrateful to quarrel too much with a book that offers so many delights to the imagination, and that is, after all, an extraordinary novelistic evocation of paradise regained. *Ada* is a novel where, to recall Milton's language about the depiction of Eden in *Paradise Lost*, nice Art has virtually assumed the role of Nature's boon pour-ing forth its inexhaustible riches, but precisely for that reason, the splendor of the achievement is marked with little spots of overripeness.

By contrast, Nabokov's control over his artistic means in both *Lolita* and *Pale Fire* seems quite flawless. In both, the re-peated allusions to poets, to conventions of the novel, to all the trappings of literary tradition, beautifully fuse with the actual fictional predicaments of the protagonists, with the way they construe their worlds. The central characters themselves, even as we see them as artful designs in words, have a poignant intensity of life that surpasses any other characterizations in Nabokov, with the exception of *Pnin*; and their cadenced, at times extravagantly figurative language is always an expression of their nature and their plight, not a self-indulgence of the author. Both novels take up the basic quixotic theme of the tortuous, teasing relation between words and things, imagination and reality. The mental and sexual proclivities of Humbert Humbert and Charles Kinbote may make them among the most bizarre heirs of the Knight of La Mancha, but the lineage is clear, down to the assumption of a *nom de combat* and the attachment to a Dulcinea by each of these literature-ridden lucid madmen. *Pale Fire*, the more formally original of the two books, may be the more culminating instance of self-consciousness in the novel because it focuses more directly on how the imagination both creates art and reflects it, and that ambiguous cyclical process of the production and reception of art is built into the novel's unique structure.

For a detailed sense of how *Lolita* works as a self-conscious fiction, I could do no better than advise the reader to consult Alfred Appel's superb introductory essay to *The Annotated Lolita*. The concluding sentence in part 1 of that essay eloquently summarizes why in both these novels fictional self-consciousness— Appel calls it involution—is able to move through the games of words and books to the urgent human predicaments equally shared by artists and ordinary mortals: "The ultimate detachment of an 'outside' view of a novel [i.e., seeing it as an artifact] inspires our wonder and enlarges our potential for compassion because, 'in the spiral unwinding of things' (a phrase from

Speak, Memory), such compassion is extended to include the mind of an author whose deeply humanistic art affirms man's ability to confront and order chaos" (p. xxxiii). Precisely how this amplitude of vision is worked out in *Pale Fire* will become clear through some attention to the details of the novel's intricate interlocking structure.

Let us recall briefly the peculiar general plan of *Pale Fire*. It begins with a brief Foreword written by one Charles Kinbote, ostensibly to introduce a 999-line poem in rhyming couplets by the prominent American poet John Francis Shade, a poem Kinbote has edited for publication after the poet's death. The text of the poem follows, and after it some 230 pages of notes by Kinbote, to which scholarly work the requisite Index is duly appended. One hardly has to read past the second note to realize that Kinbote's zany Commentary has precious little to do with the quiet meditative themes and the domestic academic settings that are the ostensible materials of the Poem. In the Commentary, Kinbote, seeing himself as the real inspiration of the Poem—indeed, as its covert subject—gradually emerges as King Charles the Beloved, hiding in exile after a revolution has taken place in the supposed European kingdom of Zembla, the magical homeland for which he constantly yearns. A victim of brilliant delusions, Kinbote, actually an émigré instructor at the small-town American university where John Shade teaches, would appear in fact to be neither Shade's intimate friend nor the king of anything, though he passionately, desperately, imagines himself to be both.

The wit and inventiveness of *Pale Fire* are so prominent in this plan that it is easy to "appreciate" the novel for the wrong reasons. On the most simplistic level, some readers have seen this as a satire on academe and a parody of the kind of exegetical erudition that Nabokov himself at the time of the book's composition was putting into his four-volume edition of *Eugene Onegin*. *Pale Fire* is of course both a satire and a parody, but to see it only as that is drastically to reduce its real scope. In quite another direction, I am afraid the novel has inspired its own Kinbotean commentators among Nabokov's critics. Exegetes of the novel, it seems to me, have tended to complicate it in gratuitous ways by publishing elaborate diagrams of its structure (which is, after all, clear enough in its main outlines), by devoting learned pages to wondering who—Nabokov, Shade, or Kinbote—is responsible for the Epigraph, by exerting their own ingenuity to demonstrate dubious theses, like the one in which both the Poem and the poet are argued to be Kinbote's inventions.

This novel is not a Jamesian experiment in reliability of narrative point of view, and there is no reason to doubt the existence of the basic fictional data—the Poem and its author, on one hand, and the mad Commentary and its perpetrator on the other, inverted left hand. The besetting sin of criticism, in any case, has been merely to uncover intricate patterns of the novel's formal games and then to assume that intricacy itself is sufficient evidence of masterful imaginative achievement. One cannot discuss this book without attending to its extraordinary ingenuity, and in a moment I shall myself go on to consider some of the elaborate tracery of its design, but the essential question to be faced is what purpose the design really serves.

Pale Fire is perhaps the most exquisitely fashioned variant of the "quixotic" novel in the French critic Marthe Robert's precise sense—a testing out through narrative invention of the double function of language as magical conjuration and radical probing, with an unblinking openness to all the moral and spiritual risks that each of those functions of language entails. It asks us, like *Don Quixote* itself, to ponder how the mind uses words to structure reality, to consider the deep trouble as well as the delights we make for ourselves through the stirring verbal realities we construct. But before trying to define any further these large issues that gradually emerge from the novel, we shall have to see how its principal mechanisms operate.

Self-conscious novels, because they are so aware of the arbitrariness of narrative conventions, tend to diverge in a variety of ways from the linear unitary structure of the usual traditional narrative; and as a result they exhibit a fondness for reproducing themselves *en abîme*, as Gide liked to say, working with Chinese-box constructions, or at least repeatedly illuminating their devious narrative ways with small replicas of the innovative structure of the whole. This practice might be traced back as far as the doublings of narrative incident in Cervantes, but its first full-scale use is easily observable in *Tristram Shandy*, where episodes like Slawkenbergius's Tale, the descent of the hot chestnut into Phutatorius's codpiece, and the several variations on the story of Trim's amour with the fair Beguine all reproduce the basic narrative operation of the whole novel: a great fuss and bother over misunderstandings permeated with hilarious double meanings hovering over a rude base of sexual fact. This kind of self-replication is more pervasive in *Pale Fire* than in any other novel by Nabokov.

The self-conscious activity of *dédoublement* and the self-conscious device of the mirror, both of which are everywhere in Nabokov's fiction, achieve a kind of apotheosis here. Reflections, real and illusory, accurate and distorted, straightforward and magical, are absolutely ubiquitous. The title, in reference to *Timon of Athens* (about which more later), refers to the moon's reflection of light from the sun. Kinbote, the supposed editor of John Shade's last poem, "Pale Fire," at once refers to it in the Foreword as a faceted crystal, and soon after strangely pauses over a vignette of the late John Shade watching a snowflake settle on his wristwatch and pensively declaring, "Crystal to crystal."[1] The Poem itself begins with an elaborate—by now, duly celebrated—image of a deceptive reflection taken for reality, compounded by the optical illusion of objects within projected outside the reflecting translucence of glass:

> I was the shadow of the waxwing slain
> By the false azure in the windowpane.
> I was the smudge of ashen fluff—and I
> Lived on, flew on, in the reflected sky.
> And from the inside, too, I'd duplicate
> Myself, my lamp, an apple on a plate:
> Uncurtaining the night, I'd let dark glass
> Hang all the furniture above the grass.

Zembla, the land of semblances that the megalomaniacal Kinbote invents to rule over in his Commentary, is a realm of mirrors. Rather like some fabulous world of science-fiction fabrication, it seems almost built of glass and reflecting surfaces. A skyscraper in its capital city is made of ultramarine glass. Most of its significant political events—strikes, conspiracies, explosions, revolutions—seem to take place in its glassworks. The names of its villains are anagrammatic mirror-reversals of the names of its heroes; most significantly, Yakob Gradus, the Zemblan assassin chosen to track down King Charles, is an ex-glazier, and the anagrammatic mirror-reversal of Sudarg of Bokay, "a mirror maker of genius" (see Index). It is worth pondering the fact that the same elements which compose the super-thug of the novel, its paradigmatic anti-aesthetic man, need but be read in the opposite direction to produce a master artist. Sudarg points toward another gifted worker in glass, a certain Rippleson—the name is suspiciously un-Zemblan—identified

in the Index as "a famous glass maker who embodied the
dapple-and-ringle play and other circular reflections on blue-
green sea water in his extraordinary stained glass windows for
the palace." The dapple-and-ringle play of circular reflections is
precisely how *Pale Fire*—Epigraph and Foreword and Poem,
Commentary, and Index—is constructed, and so the mysterious artist Rippleson looks very much like a stand-in for Vladimir Nabokov.

Circular reflections and haunting realities entrapped in the
depths of mirrors figure significantly in the body of the Poem.
The often-quoted passage at the end of Canto Three (lines
806–829) gives a general description of this "plexed artistry,"
this narrative mirroring based on "some kind / Of correlated
pattern in the game," where the poet imagines the gods in "their
involute / Abode . . . / Playing a game of worlds" with human-
kind as the pieces on the mirror-patterned chessboard. Elsewhere in the Poem, in more compressed visual imagery, Nabokov offers what amounts to a series of ideograms of the novel's
structure.

He has Shade describe an "iridule" (the word is Nabokov's
invention)—an oval cloudlet that "Reflects the rainbow in the
thunderstorm / Which in a distant valley has been staged— /
For we are most artistically caged" (lines 112–114). A moment
earlier, Shade had mentioned his Aunt Maud's "paperweight /
Of convex glass enclosing a lagoon" (lines 92–93), and a few
lines further on he recalls "The miracle of a lemniscate left /
Upon wet sand by nonchalantly deft / Bicycle tires" (lines 137–
138). This seemingly precious piece of imagery is at first
puzzling, and Kinbote of course quite misses the point in his
Commentary by citing a dictionary definition of lemniscate—"a
unicursal bicircular quartic"—then dismissing the use of the
term as an affectation. A lemniscate, however, is a continuous

figure-eight curve, which one might imagine as a figure eight lying on its side, and as such it neatly diagrams the circular, reflective relation of Commentary to Poem and Poem to Commentary. (The shape might also recall the wings of a butterfly, that inevitable Nabokovian "signature," which in fact appears again and again in the novel.) Even a rubber band on Shade's desk falls into the form of an ampersand (line 533), and a rubber band figured as an ampersand—&—is a lemniscate by another name, again the ideogram of the novel.

The Commentary and Index play their own cryptographic games with these little emblems of the novel enunciated in the Poem. There is even one instance where two ideograms are joined in a single figure, Iris Acht, the mistress of King Charles's grandfather, whose first name points back to the iridule and whose last name, "eight" in German, recalls the figure eight of the lemniscate. All this is clever enough, but like any cleverness exhibited at length, it would finally be tedious if it did not tie in as tightly as it does with the serious imaginative business of the novel, the inner life of the protagonists, the existential quandaries in which they are caught, the shimmering interplay of art and life generated by the events and the language of the narrative.

Perhaps we can begin to move beyond the commonplaces of "explicating" the devices of *Pale Fire* and get closer to the distinctive poetic reality of the novel by focusing on one particularly suggestive mirror image. Fleur, a fetching young Zemblan woman, has been sent to the palace in an appropriate state of undress to lure the homosexual prince from his inverted ways.

He awoke to find her standing with a comb in her hand before his—or rather, his grandfather's—cheval glass, a triptych of bottomless light, a really fantastic mirror, signed with

a diamond by its maker, Sudarg of Bokay. She turned about
before it: a secret device of reflection gathered an infinite number of nudes in its depths, garlands of girls in graceful and sorrowful groups, diminishing in the limpid distance, or breaking
into individual nymphs, some of whom, she murmured, must
resemble her ancestors when they were young—little peasant
garlien combing their hair in shallow water as far as the eye
could reach, and then the wistful mermaid from an old tale,
and then nothing. (pp. 111–112)

In some of the modernists, one encounters certain representations of consciousness where at the conclusion of a given moment of such representation the mind trails off, often darkly,
into nothingness. Nabokov, however, as a writer who might
perhaps be thought of as postmodernist, is less interested in the
immediacy of consciousness than in the art that creates consciousness and that, conversely, consciousness creates. The
naked Fleur surrounded by the triptych of the cheval glass is a
beautifully realized instance of the dapple-and-ringle play of
circular reflections. The glass fashioned by Sudarg of Bokay,
who as we have seen is just one remove from the fashioner of
Pale Fire, gives back not a simple image but an infinite regress
of multiplied images, and it is signed with a diamond by
Sudarg—in a lemniscate &—as Nabokov signs all his own
works with butterflies. The mirror is "fantastic" not only in the
colloquial sense of "extraordinary" but because it opens into a
whole realm of fantasy, translating a simple naked girl into the
mythological choreography of myriad dancing maidens, aptly
caught in the alliterative music of the prose—"garlands of girls
in graceful and sorrowful groups." The relation here of the reflected image to time past is particularly noteworthy. Real mirror images of course, exist only at the moment of reflection, and

so in a sense are cut off from the dimension of time. The figurative mirror of art, on the other hand, and especially of literary art, is deeply embedded in the multilayered experience of time. This is true first of all because art develops cumulatively and operates through repeated self-recapitulation, and the very medium of literary art, language, is the product of collective experience in time, suffused with the associations and recollections of times past and past literary uses. Any work of art, moreover, can exist only through an act of mediation in the consciousness of someone experiencing it, and consciousness, as the example of Joyce's technique must remind us, is essentially built up out of the infinite laminations of what the individual has seen, felt, read, fantasized in the past, however attuned he or she may be to the present moment.

The mirror itself here is a legacy of the past, not properly King Charles's but his grandfather's, the farcically named Thurgus the Turgid, who was, of course, the purple-nosed lover of Iris Acht, that hooded lady linked by appellation with circular reflections. Through the consciousness of Fleur, "murmuring" fantasies (the locution sounds like a parodic reminiscence of Virginia Woolf) as she observes herself transfigured in multiple reflection, we are moved further back in time into a legendary past where pastoral ancestors preen themselves by still waters. Recessed within that memory is a more distant one of a wistful mermaid in an old tale; and at the end of this entrancing series one glimpses the empty ground where there is neither consciousness nor art nor anything but the eternal void that both must fill if we are not to be overwhelmed by the dedication of living things to death.

The "bottomless light" of the triptych, then, ultimately leads back to the mystery implicit in the title of the novel. The pale fire of art, in the usual view, reflects the sun of reality, but we also see it here become its own sun, turning its observers, like Kinbote vis-à-vis Shade, into light-thieving moons, uncannily providing from the recesses of the assembled artifact an undying source of magical illumination for all who come to study their reflection in its surfaces. Indeed, the very first occurrence of the phrase "pale fire" in the text of the novel (p. 15), where it is attached to the incinerator burning the rejected drafts of Shade's poem, which then ascend into the air as "wind-borne black butterflies," associates the term with the refining process by which art comes into being, consuming its own impurities, and that pale fire is no reflection at all.

In a novel constructed so that reflections continually reflect other reflections, a passage like the one we have been considering becomes still more complicated when it is seen in the rings of narrative context that surround it. Though it may be a hauntingly evocative, visually memorable moment, it is, after all, no more than "the dream of a reverie," part of the pure fabrication Charles Kinbote creates of a past he never experienced in fact, in which he was king of Zembla, surrounded by futilely expectant female beauties and bevies of blooming boys. This whole fantasy, moreover, is the wildly distorted "reflection" of a poem in heroic couplets by John Shade that is in fact about other people, other places, other themes.

Self-reflexive novels tend to polarize the inherent tension between fiction and reality, then to make our perception shuttle between the poles. This procedure of polarization is given an ultimate acuteness of formulation in Kinbote's "twist[ing] and batter[ing] an apparatus criticus into the monstrous semblance of a novel" (p. 86). His tale of Zembla is manifestly a fiction twice removed from the reality in which the reader sits with book in hand, but in its vividness—witness Fleur at the mirror—in the way it manages to correspond through all its farcical gyrations to the truth of Kinbote's inner world and to the composite image of a possible European political history, it has a kind of authority, and does not allow us to dismiss it as "mere" fiction. Nabokov is particularly shrewd in the way he focuses this polarized perception through a double awareness of language as historical fact and arbitrary construct.

Zembla has its own language, a Germano-Slavic tongue (not unlike that of the imaginary country in *Bend Sinister*), and we are given frequent samples of the native lexicon, with even an occasional passage of verse quoted in the original Zemblan. There remains, moreover, some leeway of teasing ambiguity in the novel about the ultimate status of Zembla and its language. Are they purely the invention of the mad Kinbote, who is not even really Kinbote but his anagrammatic double, V. Botkin, an American scholar of Russian descent? Or, alternatively, does Kinbote's madness extend merely to his delusion that he is the exiled king of Zembla, while the existence of the country and its language, now the creation of Nabokov, not Kinbote, is assumed to be "real" within the frame of the novel? The ambiguity is, I think, a fruitful one because it prevents us from drawing simplistic conclusions about the demarcations between truth and invention within an artistic fiction. When Kinbote, then, has Fleur murmur *garlien* in the original Zemblan, the introduction of the supposedly native word serves simultaneously to authenticate the remembered scene and to remind us of its status as sheer invention, of how an author behind Kinbote is giving free play to the pleasurable impulse of making fictions, at once word-building and world-building. The double function of an artificial language is powerfully reinforced by Nabokov's numerous strategies for calling our attention, as most self-reflexive novelists have done, to the fact that the reality of the fiction is assembled from words and letters.

The Goldsworths, whose home Kinbote is renting, are perceived by their tenant as an "alphabetic family," having named their four daughters Alphina (that is, alpha), Betty (beta), Candida (is this a wry glance at Shaw?), and finally, quite simply, Dee. The books left behind in Mrs. G.'s bedroom run similarly from Amber to Zen. Kinbote informs us of three conjoined lakes near the university town known as Omega, Ozero, and Zero, thus running us backward from the ultimate end in the Greek alphabet to the point before beginnings in mathematical notation, with the Russian word for lake, *ozero*, in the middle. Ozero is also a double zero (oo), which, if the circles are tangent, is another version of a lemniscate. Outside Kinbote's Appalachia, in both the Poem and the projected world of Zembla, fictional reality exhibits a similar tendency to return to its alphabetic origins. The immediate line of succession in the Zemblan royal family is King Alphin (the masculine form of Alphina), Queen Blenda, King Charles (who is Charles II, a "successor" in role to Charles I, the deposed and executed king of England, but also Charles Xavier, that is, Charles X, the unknown one in this alphabet soup of a novel). In Shade's poem, skaters cross the frozen Lake Omega from Exe to Wye, and again in Kinbote's bizarre version of the Shade household, the mysterious alphabetical powers exert such dominance that Mrs. Shade even suffers from an alphabetically determined allergy, to artichokes, avocado pears, African acorns, and so forth. Finally, all this patterning down of narrative materials into alphabetical schemata jibes perfectly with the prominent importance of anagrams in the novel. Anagrams, here joined with a transformational variant, word golf (q.v., Index), are a perennial passion of the Scrabble-playing Nabokov; but here more than in any other of his novels they make fine thematic sense by demonstrating language's capacity for mirror-reversal, by showing how the universal elements of written language can be manipulated by the artificer through a constant chain of shifting patterns so that they make, or at least designate, different, even antithetical, realities.

These reminders of the alphabetic constituents of the novel's reality are thematically complemented, on a higher level of complexity, by the reiterated imagery in which the things of this world turn into verse and literary convention or, conversely, by which literature with its formal norms makes itself into a habitable world. John Shade invites his wife to enter with him into a secret geography of poetry and intellectual design, "Empires of rhyme, Indies of calculus" (line 602), and the first extended image of his poem after that initial reflection in and through the poet's window is of a *paysage littéraire*, of a landscape transmuted into literature:

> Whose spurred feet have crossed
> From left to right the blank page of the road?
> Reading from left to right in winter's code:
> A dot, an arrow pointing back; repeat:
> Dot, arrow pointing back . . . A pheasant's feet!
>   (lines 20–24)

The image archly forces us to do a double take: we envisage the winter landscape—of course, conveyed to us in a poem by a fictional poet in a novel—at the same time that we see we are reading a printed page from left to right in which a series of conventional symbols encodes a meaning that we must decipher. All communication is a code, poetry being simply the most complex, integrated ordering of encoding elements. Kinbote's mad Commentary represents an extreme instance, at once moving and farcical, of the general difficulty of decoding such artful texts: he puts together Appalachia, waxwing, crystal land and gets . . . Zembla, revolution, a stalking assassin. Shade, having begun his poem by transforming a landscape into printer's ink on a white page, concludes it, after the various musings on plexed artistry and games of worlds, by elevating the ordering idea of the writer's art, with some qualification, to a cosmic principle:

> . . . I feel I understand
> Existence, or at least a minute part
> Of my existence, only through my art,
> In terms of combinational delight;
> And if my private universe scans right,
> So does the verse of galaxies divine
> Which I suspect is an iambic line. (lines 970–976)

This poet's vision of an iambic cosmos is offered tentatively, wistfully, by a man whose lifelong vocation has been to achieve coherence through the formal symmetries of language, but one begins to see concretely what Alfred Appel means when he describes art in Nabokov as the model of how we confront and order chaos. Shade is pursued by the idea of death, the extinction of the self, and he tries to imagine poetry as a vehicle of transcendence. On the other side of the mirror, Kinbote is pursued by his own derangement ("the frozen mud and horror in my heart" [p. 258]), that is, a radical isolation of the self, and his way out is the Poem with which he thinks he has "impregnated" Shade, his means of shaping the private chaos and terror of his experience, and entering through art into the human community. A latter-day Quixote, he aspires to become a hero of literature not by deed but by talk alone. In point of fact, Kinbote's real poem is the novel he builds out of Shade's poem in his Commentary, interpretation turned creation. "I can do what only a true artist can do," Kinbote justifiably boasts toward the end, "pounce upon the forgotten butterfly of revelation, wean myself abruptly from the habit of things, see the web of the world, and the warp and the weft of the web" (p. 289). The imagery of warp and weft takes us back to the "link-and-bobolink," the "correlated pattern in the game" of Shade's poem (lines 812–813), at the same time that it parodically exaggerates in Kinbote, a mad version of a Nabokovian artist, Nabokov's own fondness for alliterative effects.

Kinbote immediately continues these alliterative flourishes in language that is expressively lurid, marked by lambent iambs, in consonance with his own sensibility and situation, as he recalls the theme of deciphering enunciated in Canto One of the Poem and joins an image of pale fire to the novel's emblematic association of art with entomology. Clutching the poet's index cards, "I found myself enriched with an indescribable amazement as if informed that fire-flies were making decodable signals on behalf of stranded spirits, or that a bat was writing a legible tale of torture in the bruised and branded sky." Clearly, Kinbote himself is the stranded spirit par excellence, but in his mental and social alienation he merely embodies an extreme instance of the role of isolate in which every human being is to some degree cast. The pattern-making process of decoding art into art is an ultimate necessity: without it the spirit is lost forever.

Pale Fire urges the idea of art as the sole way of coping with chaos—Shade, coolly and ironically, Kinbote, desperately— but the idea is sharply qualified with a philosophical realism by the steady awareness that any poetic invention is, after all, a farrago of words, a delusional system, a form of madness. The title of Shade's critical study of Pope, *Supremely Blest*, refers us to a passage in the *Essay on Man* (2:267–270) crucial to the plan of the novel, and though the relevant lines have been duly brought forth by previous critics of *Pale Fire*, beginning after its initial publication with Mary McCarthy, they are particularly worth reflecting on in the present connection:

> See the blind beggar dance, the cripple sing,
> The sot a hero, lunatic a king;
> The starving chemist in his golden views
> Supremely blest, the poet in his Muse.

The conjunction of lunatic king and poet is of course the conjunction in the novel of those antithetical doubles, Kinbote and Shade. There is, moreover, a thematic rather than a structural revelation about the novel in Pope's tartly satirical yoking, shrewdly reinforced by a rare enjambement, of the starving chemist (that is, alchemist) and the poet. The alchemist deludes himself by thinking he can effect a magical transformation of lead to gold (in the novel, Kinbote, no doubt with the art of Sudarg and Rippleson in mind, refers to writing as "blue magic"). The poet, for Nabokov's purposes at any rate, deludes himself by imagining he can transform the death-sodden mire of existence into a pellucid artifice of eternity. But perhaps, we are made to feel through both "Pale Fire" and its Commentary, the delusion is strictly necessary to make life livable; perhaps in some way it is not altogether a delusion. Kinbote's *apparatus criticus* strongly confirms this double sense of poetry as delusion and ordering truth by repeatedly drawing attention to how real-seeming characters are laid out on a grid of literary coordinates, so that at moments those literary coordinates seem almost to constitute an autonomous reality. In a dream of King Charles—that is, the dream of a dream of a dream—the neglected queen is imagined assuming a variety of destinies, including that of becoming a character in a novel (p. 212). Sylvia

O'Donnell, a fashionable and much-married supporter of the king, is said to be in the process of divorcing her latest mate "when last seen in this Index" (p. 311). Most centrally, Jakob Gradus, who in the perspective of Kinbote's novelistic omniscience becomes progressively more "real," down to an X-ray view of the partly digested french fries and ham sandwich roiling his insides, is constituted again and again wholly through the rhythms and rules of a poem where, of course, he never really appears:

> We shall accompany Gradus in constant thought, as he makes his way from distant dim Zembla to green Appalachia, through the entire length of the poem, following the road of its rhythm, riding past in a rhyme, skidding around the corner of a run-on, breathing with the caesura, swinging down to the foot of the page from line to line as from branch to branch, hiding between two words (see note to line 596), reappearing on the horizon of a new canto, steadily marching nearer in iambic motion, crossing streets, moving up with his valise on the escalator of the pentameter, stepping off, boarding a new train of thought, entering the hall of a hotel, putting out the bedlight, while Shade blots out a word, and falling asleep as the poet lays down his pen for the night. (p. 78)

This leaves the assassin Gradus—"tree" in Zemblan to the poet's Shade—as a potent metrical illusion, now you see him, now you don't, whose ambiguous existence projected onto the lines of a printed page by a madman forces us to ponder the reality of fictional things. As a "fact" within the novel, he is of course the product of sheer delusion, what Kinbote's fantasies have made out of a murderer named Jack Gray sentenced by

Kinbote's landlord, Judge Goldsworth. And yet the manifest fictionality of Gradus's existence does nothing to diminish the progressive power of his presence in the novel; and set between the two poets, one happily heterosexual and lucidly witty, the other haplessly homosexual and darkly melodramatic, the political assassin makes the most cogent thematic and even historical sense. He is the consummate embodiment of anti-imagination, asexual (he has tried to castrate himself), impervious to the pleasures of the body as of the spirit, the perfect political man of the modern totalitarian state, a gross obedient goon with a gun in his hand. One sees in his delineation the utter seriousness that underlies the playfulness of Nabokov's fictional games. The trauma of the murder of the writer's own father by Russian fascists, compounded by his brother's death at the hands of the Nazis, has haunted him throughout his career, and he may play with assassinations and related political acts, but he does not toy with them.

In order to see more fully how *Pale Fire* opens up perspectives on the luminous circularity of reflective relations between poetry and reality, it is important to observe that not only is the novel built upon the reversed images of two different kinds of poet but that the two figures repeatedly allude to two antithetical English poets, and through them to the two opposite poles of English poetry. The poetic ascendancy of Shade's "Pale Fire" of course belongs to Alexander Pope. Shade is an academic specialist in Pope; he casts his poem in Popean couplets, divides it into four cantos like the *Essay on Man*, uses his verse, like the *Essay*, to discourse philosophically on man's estate, stretching his iambs, like Pope's, to the starry spaces, and speculating, like Pope, on a possible afterlife and its effects on the here-and-now (see, for example, *The Essay on Man*, 4:173–180). Pope, too, published a poem with a hilariously addled Commentary much longer than the original text, the *Dunciad Variorum*, and the theme of that poem, described in the 1728 preface as "the restoration of the reign of Chaos and Night," could easily characterize what happens politically and personally in the Commentary to John Shade's poem.

In any event, it is obvious that the texture of Shade's poem and its informing sensibility are far from Popean, despite the Popean prosody, but the disparity is quite to the point, for *Pale Fire* is in part about how literature reuses literature, assimilates it, and makes something strange and new out of it. Thus the twentieth-century colloquial rhythms of "Pale Fire"—an eighteenth-century critic would have called them "nerveless"—constantly work against the formal emphases and tensions of the traditional couplet form, often producing an effect of studied gaucherie (though there may also be some awkwardness that is inadvertent). Some of the verbal clowning reminds one not of Pope but of his great Romantic admirer, the improvisatory Byron of *Don Juan*. There is real wit in the Poem, but it is Nabokovian, not Popean, in its intense visuality and its flaunted ingenuity (for example, a blurry movie close-up rerun on TV is "a soft form dissolving in the prism / Of corporate desire" [lines 456–457]). This image of course reflects the way television sets turned off in the available technology of the 1950s. At its brilliant best, the Poem, however philosophical, achieves a most un-Popean effect: poignancy. Vividly focusing the particulars of sensory experience taken from a familiar everyday world, and reveling in the gorgeousness of words, sounds, and imagery, it transmutes the heroic couplet into the distinctive handiwork of the writer who invented Adam Krug, Humbert Humbert, and Pnin:

Nor can one help the exile, the old man
Dying in a motel, with the loud fan
Revolving in the torrid prairie night
And, from the outside, bits of colored light
Reaching his bed like dark hands from the past
Offering gems; and death is coming fast.
He suffocates and conjures in two tongues
The nebulae dilating in his lungs. (lines 609–616)

What John Shade does to Pope is but a modest intimation of what Charles Kinbote does to John Shade. If Shade is a "Popean" poet (we have seen the necessity for the quotation marks), Kinbote, mulling over Shade's poem, becomes a "Shakespearean" one—in the old antithesis, Shakespeare as the untamed, enormously fecund genius over against the polished wit operating ingeniously within limited scope. A passage from Pope gives us the conjunction of the lunatic and the poet, but Shakespeare (in *Midsummer Night's Dream*) tells us that the poet, the madman, and the lover are one, and of course Kinbote is all three. His world bristles with reminders of the Bard, and even his name, transmogrified in the novel into the Elizabethan "bodkin," recalls the most famous of Shakespeare's soliloquies. Though the name Zembla is lifted from Pope, that dim distant country is thoroughly Shakespeareanized in Kinbote's presentation of it. As a young prince, Charles Xavier rents rooms in Coriolanus Lane. His Scottish tutor, Mr. Campbell, is fond of reciting all of *Macbeth* by heart. Conmal, the prince's uncle, devotes half a century to the translation of Shakespeare's complete works. (It is Conmal's translation of *Timon of Athens* that Kinbote happens to have with him on his last retreat "like Timon in his cave" to a rural cabin.) Even the name Shakespeare is attributed to a Zemblan place name, Shalksbore, meaning "knave's farm." On the Appalachian side of things, Wordsmith (which is to say "poet") University boasts a famous avenue lined with all the trees mentioned in Shakespeare, and which Kinbote takes the trouble to enumerate. The account in Shade's poem of Hazel Shade's suicide leads the commentator in his note to line 463 into a Hamlet-like soliloquy on suicide. Both Ophelia and a bare botkin ("note the correct spelling," Kinbote tells us) are mentioned, while ironically, this self-designated Christian prince whose throne has been usurped comes out in defense of suicide, thus providing us one of several inverted reflections of Shakespeare.

Though the extravagances of Kinbote's paranoid megalomania lead to florid excesses in style, as we have seen and as we shall see, there nevertheless is something Shakespearean about the poetry he makes out of his madness when one compares it to the Poem by John Shade. Shade writes poetry out of his musings, a poetry always bound to his immediate personal experience, however large a metaphysical background he may set behind it. Kinbote, on the other hand, is able to create a whole world with a history, a politics, a class structure, a set of folk traditions, and to people it with dramatically vivid figures. Soaring beyond the ordinariness of everyday things, his imagination delights in conjuring up traditional literary materials like exiled princes, palace intrigues, secret underground passageways, assassinations, beautiful noble ladies, and grotesque clowns.

In this way the novel, with its "Popean" poem and its "Shakespearean" commentary, generates a genuinely binocular vision, showing forth in intricate interplay two kinds of poetry, two modes of imagination, that mark the opposite ends of the field within which literary creation is free to play. Shakespeare, moreover, is repeatedly involved in the theme of translation that is one of the conceptual keys of the novel. Shakespeare, always the supreme poet of the Western tradition for Nabokov—see, for example, how he is spoken of and allusively used in *Bend Sinister*—offers in his richness the ultimate instance of the constant sea changes poetry suffers in the consciousness of the readers it needs in order to exist at all. Shade's advice to college students on the reading of Shakespeare, recorded by Kinbote in Boswellian fashion, intimates the consummate power of the master poet but offers no real practical guidance for the challenge of assimilating him: the student should "get drunk on the poetry of *Hamlet* or *Lear*, . . . read with his spine and not with his skull." (This is almost verbatim what Nabokov used to advise his Cornell students.)

Shade, of course, has no idea that his own last poem will be subjected by Kinbote to a reading from the base of the spine and the floor of the psyche. King Charles's first experience of Shakespeare is through the mediation of Uncle Conmal's translations, and the most hilariously revealing comment on the accuracy of those translations comes in the last words of Conmal, whose English was self-taught: "*Comment dit-on 'mourir' en anglais?*" Every literary work, even in a language one can read, must be inwardly "translated" by each of its readers, and all translations are, necessarily, mistranslations, differing only in the direction and relative absurdity of their inaccuracies. Sybil Shade's French translations of Marvell and Donne are stigmatized by the jealous Kinbote. For his part, he admits to having translated some of Shade's poetry into Zemblan some twenty years previously, but if the accuracy of the "translation" that his Commentary provides is any indication, one is happy to be spared these juvenile gems.

Communications between various members of the Extremist secret service are a farce of mistranslations. A telephone conversation between Gradus and his superiors, in which both sides have forgotten the code and speak their own versions of broken English, offers a perfect paradigm of the translation problem: "Each side, finally, had forgotten the meaning of certain phrases pertaining to the other's vocabulary so that in result, their tangled and expensive talk combined charades with an obstacle race in the dark." More laughably, a sentence written in "governess English" by Queen Disa to the king after the revolution—"I want you to know that no matter how much you hurt me, you cannot hurt my love" (p. 205)—is intercepted, converted into crude Zemblan by a Hindu (!) Extremist, and rendered back in English by Kinbote as: "I desire you and love when you flog me." Oddly enough, this howler is not altogether pointless, since there is surely an element of masochism in Disa's futilely persistent love for the neglectful king, so even an outrageous mistranslation (like Kinbote's Commentary) may turn up an unsuspected face of the truth.

It should be observed that a translation from English to Zemblan and back to English again is a circular reflection, which, as we have already seen through other images, is what this novel is all about. The most pointed double translation, of course, is the text from *Timon of Athens* (4.3.439–443) that supplies the title of the novel. The original lines, never actually quoted, sketch out a cosmic cycle of universal theft, everything working at a distance to borrow its light or force from something else, and completely transforming what it takes:

> The sun's a thief, and with his great attraction
> Robs the vast sea; the moon's an arrant thief,
> And her pale fire she snatches from the sun;
> The sea's a thief, whose liquid surge resolves
> The moon into salt tears.

Now, Kinbote quotes his own re-Englished version of Conmal's Zemblan translation of these lines, without, however, suspecting that they contain the phrase "pale fire." Since *Timon of Athens* in its Zemblan transmogrification is the only Shakespeare he has with him in his cabin, he aptly observes that his "luck would have been a statistical monster" if Shade's title had appeared in that particular play. The irony of Kinbote's ignorance on this, and many other, points reminds us of the crucial difference between poetry and statistics, of how much Kinbote is the creature, in a sense the prisoner, of Nabokov's combinatorial art. The only lines Kinbote actually quotes anywhere in the novel from Conmal's *Timon* are, of course, just those that contain the title phrase, safely buried under the debris of translation and retranslation:

> The sun is a thief: she lures the sea and robs it.
> The moon is a thief: he steals his silvery light from
>   the sun.
> The sea is a thief: it dissolves the moon.

There is distortion but obviously no dapple-and-ringle play in this circular reflection. What it presents us with is a model of the lower limits of translation. Some literal sense of the imagery is preserved, though one might note that in the inverted reflection of the original, the genders of sun and moon are reversed; but this crude, flat-footed version destroys the dancing music of the verse, the emotional coloring of the language, the dramatized mystery of interplay among heavenly and earthly bodies—in short, the poetry of the passage. Furthermore, the sudden and arresting pulse of pathos in the conceit of the last two lines—"whose liquid surge resolves / The moon into salt tears"—is lopped off by the ridiculous and abrupt "it dissolves the moon."

The gauche mistranslation of this passage, then, serves as a counterpoint to the splendid mistranslation effected through the Commentary, where pathos is wonderfully twinned with absurdity, and the poetry of nostalgia for a lost world vivifies the fantasy images and imbues the prose with sumptuous life. The life of the prose, to be precise, is extravagant, in perfect keeping with Kinbote's flamboyant nature and his sense of his own plight. The wild energy with which his language joins disparate realms and transforms things through metaphor is another measure of its "Shakespearean" quality. Here is Kinbote at the outset, in the Foreword, putting us on notice about the kind of sensibility with which we are to be confronted in this narrative: "Mr. and Mrs. Shade . . . were having trouble with their old Packard in the slippery driveway where it emitted whines of agony but could not extricate one tortured rear wheel out of a concave inferno of ice" (p. 20). Anyone who has ever got a car caught in snow and heard the awful shriek of tires spinning in icy ruts will recognize the experience, but however sharply observed, the experience has been transposed by metaphor into the special key of Kinbote's inner world. In this extreme application of personification, everything has been stepped up—whines of agony, tortured wheels, an inferno of ice—into an externalized image of Kinbote's own writhing sense of entrapment. The imagination at work here is a powerful one, but, as it will proceed to do on a much larger scale in the Commentary, it insists on refashioning the outer world as an embodiment of its acute interior distress. The image of imprisonment in ice, moreover, is linked with the novel's emblematic images of being caught in crystal, buried in the depths of a mirror.

Such use of figurative language is complicated and enriched by a certain flickering critical awareness in Kinbote of how the

choice of imagery transforms the object and constitutes a literary act. In describing, for example, the "actual" imprisonment
of Charles Xavier, he adopts the following figure to represent
the tired king's vision of his card-playing captors: "The King
yawned, and the illumined card players shivered and dissolved
in the prism of his tears" (p. 123). The metaphor has the studied
quality of a conceit that characterizes a good deal of Kinbote's
style, but the conceit very precisely focuses an understanding
of how the refracting medium of perception frames, distorts,
dramatically reshapes the objects perceived. Needless to say,
the prism in the bleary eye of the beholder is continuous with
the sundry crystals, rippled glass, and iridules that provide
models in miniature of how the novel as a whole works, something underscored by the fact that the source of illumination
referred to here is a lantern around which lepidopterist Nabokov sets flapping a signatory moth.

As even these brief examples may suggest, Kinbote's prose
delights in extravagance, but it is the extravagance of a wildly
original observer who tries to place critical distance between
his own perceptions and the exaggerated formulas of second-
rate literature. The enlivening ironic intelligence, in other
words, behind the novel as a whole works as a pale reflection in
Kinbote, intermittently and most imperfectly, but sufficiently
to provide little critical checks on the wonderful but outrageous
excesses of his narrative. In describing Fleur, for example, he
cites the view of her lover, Otar, who "said that when you walked
behind her, the swing and play of those slim haunches was
something intensely artistic, something Arab girls were taught
in special schools by special Parisian panders who were after-
wards strangled" (p. 128). Kinbote, however, is quick to put
down this and related notions in the immediate context as
"rather kitschy prattle." As generally happens with parody,

he—and the reader with him—manages to have it both ways, reveling in the rich absurdity of pseudo-exotica and seeing the absurdity for what it is.

One has only to compare a moment like this with the luridly illuminated scenes in Egyptian houses of child prostitution in Lawrence Durrell's *Justine* to see the difference between a novel where fictional self-consciousness is continuous and one where it is at best episodic. Durrell's *Quartet*, of course, is self-conscious in being a fiction about the writing of novels that experiments with different points of view and deploys several different novelists-within-the-novel. Nevertheless, it is hard to read long stretches of it except as highly colored set pieces or entertainments in which Durrell's own enjoyment of kitschy prattle tends to extinguish his critical consciousness of the problematic relationship between literature and reality. In *Pale Fire*, by contrast, that authorial consciousness never falters, and Nabokov achieves a still more difficult thing by making parody work for him as he repeatedly goes beyond it. That is, Kinbote's prose includes a good many parodic elements that aptly serve as means of inadvertent self-characterization or self-incrimination; however, the writing here is not in the least restricted to parody but creates a sumptuous poetry of its own, an original imaginative confection studded with parodic plums.

The shrewd double nature of Kinbote's prose is particularly palpable in those passages where he comes out most explicitly as a spokesman for the poetic imagination, as in the following reflection, triggered by thinking of the thug Gradus's dismally limited world:

> How much happier the wide-awake indolents, the monarchs among men, the rich monstrous brains deriving intense enjoyment and rapturous pangs from the balustrade of a terrace

at nightfall, from the lights and the lake below, from the distant mountain shapes melting into the dark apricot of the afterglow, from the black conifers outlined against the pale ink of the zenith, and from the garnet and green flounces of the water along the silent, sad, forbidden shoreline. Oh my sweet Boscobel! And the tender and terrible memories, and the shame, and the glory, and the maddening intimations, and the star that no party member can ever reach. (p. 232)

A good deal of this is surely meant to be taken quite seriously. Nabokov's work as far back as the 1930s embodies a double perception of the artist as a monarch among men and, perhaps more prominently, as a vulnerable freak, and Kinbote-Charles is both. The whole Commentary is manifestly the product of a richly monstrous brain anxiously pursuing the memory of a cherished past through the verbal evocation of its concrete details. The precise painterly composition here of the remembered scene in line, color, and mass—the dark apricot horizon, the pale ink of the zenith, the black outline of the conifers, the green and garnet borders of the lake—is not the meandering of a madman but Nabokov's artful prose at its best. (No detail wasted, the pale ink brings us back to the motif of landscape as writing or drawing, while the garnet and green invoke the elaborate game of reds and greens played across the two parts of the novel.) Then, with the exclamation "Oh my sweet Boscobel!" the passage swings into open parody, tripping on through those emptily rhetorical "ands" not only to a parody of best-seller kitsch—"and the shame and the glory"—but also to a parody of one of Nabokov's favorite stylistic effects: the delicately beautiful alliteration of "apricot of the afterglow" and "garnet and green flounces" is crudely mimicked in the vapid cliché, "tender and terrible."

Remarkably, Kinbote can be made to pirouette on parody and move a step beyond it to complete the initial statement about the poet and his experience. "Maddening intimations" is a phrase that straddles, almost seeming to belong to the string of best-seller clichés yet pointing past it to a complex sense of how the sensuous poetic imagination responds in recollection to the aching sweetness of what it has undergone. "The star that no party member can reach" then exhibits a kind of serious wit clearly beyond the immediately preceding series of banalities, and it marks a moment quite free of irony. For a brief but significant instant, the sense of life of Vladimir Nabokov, exiled novelist, makes full contact with that of the exiled king, this fantasy of a fantasy of the author's, and we glimpse the alignment between the fictionally refracted lost land of Zembla and a land on the real map, poignantly remembered but forever closed to one of its great writers.

It is worth recalling in this connection these lines from "An Evening of Russian Poetry," a poem Nabokov wrote in English in the 1940s: "Beyond the seas where I have lost my scepter / I hear the neighing of dappled nouns, / soft participles coming down the steps, / treading on leaves, trailing their rustling gowns."[2]

We have seen how all such affirmations of faith in poetry and the superiority of the creative imagination are qualified by context—here, at the penultimate moment of the affirmation, by the inset of parody. What gives *Pale Fire* its fullness of statement about the ambiguous interlacing of imagination and reality, what makes it finally a major achievement in the tradition of the self-reflexive novel, is that these dialectical qualifications are translated into the novel's most basic facts of character and plot. Charles Xavier, the tender-hearted homosexual king fleeing from Extremist blackguards, is a wonderful creation, however bizarre, and even when we "reconstruct" the novel and realize that he is the fantasy of Charles Kinbote, we are hardly prepared to give him up, to discount as mere fabrication the reality he and his native land have come to assume: finally, the king is more real as an imaginatively felt presence than Kinbote, who in turn is more real, by virtue of the narrative structure itself, than John Shade.

But the central paradox is pursued deep into the recessed interior of the novel. Kinbote as Charles Xavier is a "Shakespearean" poet realizing his dreams, which are made to seem bolder, more exciting and revealing, than the drab stuff of everyday waking reality. And yet, Charles (or Kinbote as Charles) is also the prisoner of his dreams, painfully incapable of acting in fact by his very addiction to acting in imagination.

Kinbote's homosexuality, as several critics have observed, provides an "inverted" image of the heterosexual Shade, but I think we should not rule out some psychological interest in the phenomenon on the part of Nabokov, for all his forays against Freud. There is, at least as he appears to see it, at any rate, a certain element of narcissism in the homosexual (or, perhaps one must hasten to say, in *this* homosexual), who can love only one or another variation of his own reflected physical image. If Kinbote-Charles embodies what Coleridge called the "esemplastic" power of the poetic imagination, he also illustrates the painfully narcissistic danger of being a poet, who may be unable to make contact at the most crucial moments with something outside of and different in kind from himself. This whole aspect of the fantasied king is most vividly evident in the unconsummated relationship with his queen. Her full name is Paradisa, but she is only Disa to him, the paradise from which his own nature excludes him. The interesting point made is that Charles is far from indifferent to Disa. He is sensitive enough to feel her frustrated love for him, and he would like to love her, actually does love her in a kind of repeated interior gesture, a wishful imagining. Whenever he is confronted, however, with her flesh-and-blood presence, the concrete fact of her otherness as woman, he hastily withdraws into his safe circle of pliant boys.

The most revealing moment in this process comes in his last meeting with her, at her Riviera villa, after his flight into exile. "He was, had always been," the king thinks back on his relationship with his wife, "casual and heartless. But the heart of his dreaming self, both before and after the rupture, made extraordinary amends" (p. 209). Nabokov, though at times troubled or intrigued by the idea of solipsism, is finally an antisolipsist, and here, as in Humbert's treatment of Lolita, he clearly sees that one's dreams, however beautiful, may make someone else their helpless victim if they are one's only chart to a human reality that is, after all, peopled by many souls, each with its own needs and prerogatives. Kinbote broadens the implications of the observed contradiction by immediately going on to talk of dreams as poetry: "These heart-rending dreams transformed the drab prose of his feelings for her into strong and strange poetry, subsiding undulations of which would flash and disturb him throughout the day, bringing back the pang and the richness— and then only the pang, and then only its glancing reflection— but not affecting at all his attitude toward the real Disa." The movement of undulations, flashing and diminishing reflections, returns us to the dapple-and-ringle play of Rippleson's mirrors and thus to the structure of the novel as a whole, so the scope of the critical judgment expressed reaches to the limits of *Pale Fire*'s world, where a "reality" of strong and strange poetry is elaborately constructed as a means of evading reality.

The dialectic swing here from thesis to antithesis is even translated into the rhythms of the prose. As the sentence describes the king's dreamworld of poetry, it catches us up poetically in a pronounced rhythm that deftly imitates the process described—subsiding undulations and fading reflections. Then, after the second dash, there is a break from the mimetic music to a plain prose-rhythm that reveals the unadorned truth beyond Charles's private poem, that none of this passionate dreaming affected the king's attitude toward the real Disa as we see, in what might be described as an anti-epiphany, a moment of seeming revelation that proves to be a moment of revealing delusion.

The king, bidding his wife a last farewell, holds her in his arms at her request, feeling her as "a limp, shivering ragdoll." Then he begins to walk off from the villa. On an impulse, he turns to look back toward Disa, a "white figure with the listless grace of ineffable grief" seen in the distance bending over a garden table, "and suddenly a fragile bridge was suspended between waking indifference and dream-love." But the bridge is more than tenuous, it is illusory, for the addiction to dreams is not so easily broken, and he who regards life from a distance, always through an interior prism, as the king regards Disa, as Kinbote peering through windows and blinds regards Shade, is apt to fall prey to optical illusion. The bending figure moves, "and he saw it was not at all she but poor Fleur de Fyler collecting the documents left among the tea things" (p. 214).

The poignancy of this moment when the spell of the dream breaks illustrates how a fiction focused on the dynamic of fiction-making can address itself not merely to the paradoxes of the writer's craft but to the ambiguities of the human condition. *Pale Fire* is, I would contend, finally a philosophic novel in the same sense one can apply the term to Diderot and Sterne: its principal concern, moving through literature beyond literature, is with how each individual mind filters reality, re-creates it, and with the moral quandaries generated by that problematic of epistemology. In the metaparodic form of this novel, moreover, as in *Lolita*, Nabokov has overcome the weakness to which his earliest fiction—like *King, Queen, Knave* or *The Eye*—tends of producing characters who are perhaps too much *fantouches*, mere manipulated puppets. Of the cast of characters here, at least Kinbote, John Shade, Hazel Shade, and Disa have enough interiority, enough seeming autonomy as "living" figures, to engage us as more than ingenious fabrications, to reflect in the bizarrely cut facets of their existence the contradictions of our own.

In a way, *Pale Fire* is the most somber of Nabokov's involuted fictions. Both of his novels on totalitarian states, *Invitation to a Beheading* and *Bend Sinister*, end by breaking through a hole in the fictional fabric from a world that has become a death trap into the artist's serene realm of freedom. In *Pale Fire*, on the other hand, the splendid edifice of poetic illusion is more seriously undercut by an exposure of the perils of involvement in such illusion, and the very end of the novel zigzags between artifice and reality and alternative artifice in a manner that allows no clear way out. "My notes and self are petering out," Kinbote tells us at the beginning of the third paragraph from the end, yet he and the terrors of his world are not simply cast aside as a used-up fictional hypothesis. He does, to be sure, intimate that he could become Vladimir Nabokov on the other side of the fictional fabric, or that he might direct and act in another kind of fiction, a swashbuckling film to be called *Escape from Zembla*. He also offers a final hint of the "real" plot of *Pale*

Fire by imagining he might devise a melodramatic play in which one lunatic (Jack Grey) pursuing another lunatic (Kinbote) accidentally kills a poet. But, most instructively, the concluding moment of the novel belongs to Gradus or, rather, to Kinbote's vision of "a bigger, more respectable, more competent Gradus," moving steadily across the map toward his victim with sudden death in his bulging pocket. The circuit of fictional illusion, just broken, is resumed at the very end as Kinbote's paranoia once more asserts itself: the last voice we hear is again, clearly and urgently, the voice of the hunted king.

The fantasies of the fictional character Kinbote, however, also show a troubling correspondence to historical fact, weirdly refracted but also startlingly focused through the prism of art. *Pale Fire*, written after half a century of violent revolution, world war, totalitarian terror, and the genocidal slaughter of millions—an epidemic of barbarity profoundly shaking the personal life of the novelist—is very much a self-conscious novel of our times. Its display of the writer's blue magic of word-and-image play is a dazzling delight; its affirmation of the abiding beauty of life in the imagination is brilliantly enacted in the fiction, but after the last glitter of the prestidigitator's implements, it is the shadow of the assassin that falls on the final page.

There is, nevertheless, still one more dialectical turn in the paradoxical interplay between fiction and reality. Gradus's grim name occupies the very last moment of the main consecutive narrative, but it is the Index that actually completes the book, which ends with the words "Zembla, a distant northern land," taking us away from the stalking killer and the politics of terror back into the mists of the imagination where enchanted realms are created and poems are begun. We do not surrender the imagination, but on our way to this ultimate point we have come to see the drastic costs and limits of living by it alone. Our vision of the imagination, through the history-haunted quixotism of this self-reflexive novel, has been both enlarged and subtly, somberly transformed; and that is precisely what the novelistic enterprise, from the seventeenth century to our own age, has at its best achieved.

5

Autobiography as Alchemy in *Pale Fire*

There is an obvious sense in which autobiography has no relevance to Nabokov's fiction, and he would have been the first to denounce any pursuit of links between an author's life and his work as the pedantry of minds too dull to respond to the intrinsic enchantment of fictional invention. Again and again in his interviews and obiter dicta, Nabokov insisted on the distance between himself and his protagonists, and on the status of all his novels as consciously wrought artifacts, constituting new worlds and not reflecting the conventionally presupposed one that he and his readers were said to inhabit. Purposeful, exquisite design, not "self-expression," is the watermark on every page he published. When the novelist Herbert Gold asked him in an interview whether his characters sometimes took on a recalcitrant life of their own, he responded in a combination of Johnsonian peremptoriness and Nabokovian punning, "My characters are galley slaves."[1]

This is precisely what has irritated many readers. Nabokov certainly was, as David Bethea has put it in contemporary American idiom, "a control freak"—and this is the ultimate source of his detestation of Freud, who wanted to see an essential connection between unconscious mental processes and artistic creativity. But if novel-writing is actually performed as the exercise of perfect control over zestfully invented fictional constructs, can there be any purchase for biographical criticism? Nabokov's commentators have by and large focused on the elaboration of design in the fiction, as, recently, Vladimir Alexandrov has done on metaphysical grounds in *Nabokov's Otherworld*, or as even Nabokov's authoritative biographer, Brian Boyd, has done in the critical sections of his admirable two-volume study, working on the assumption that if we patiently attend to the design we will come to appreciate the nuanced, luminous intelligence that informs the design. My own previous discussion of *Pale Fire* is clearly based on this same assumption.

Pale Fire represents the supreme deployment of design among Nabokov's novels, and precisely in this regard it has been a source of annoyance to unsympathetic readers and of continuing fascination to readers sympathetically disposed. Miles of printer-ribbon have been worn out in expounding the intricacies of relation among Epigraph, Foreword, Poem, Commentary, and Index; the play of mirror images and other kinds of mirrorings; the sundry alphabetic games and anagrammatic cryptograms; the recurrence and transmutation of motifs; the winding thread of allusions to Pope, Shakespeare, and the historical Charles II. Some such attention to all these appears in the previous chapter of the present book.

I do not mean to suggest that any of this extravagant ingenuity on the part of the novelist is irrelevant to a reading of the novel. On the contrary, if you don't relish word games and codes and teasingly concealed patterns, and if you don't enjoy the exuberance of sheer fictional invention—a fictitious American state and university, and a far more fictitious European country with its language, folklore, and poetry—you are liable to toss away *Pale Fire* in thorough impatience before you get halfway through. Optimally, this profusion of patterning leads a reader to ponder productively such topics as literature and its perilous dependence on interpretation, the varieties of mimesis, language, and what we suppose to be reality, freedom and fatedness, coincidence and design, the relation between this world and any imagined world to come. In all this, Nabokov emerges as a seriously philosophic novelist—quite rightly, I think— consciously concerned with questions of aesthetics, epistemology, ontology, and metaphysics that have no obvious and direct connection with the particular circumstances of his own life.

It nevertheless seems to me that what finally makes *Pale Fire* more than the cleverest piece of fictional cryptography in the English language is that it bears so palpably the weight of its author's personal experience. Despite Nabokov's excessive admiration for Alain Robbe-Grillet's elegant experiments in fictional constructivism, he was not himself—at least in one essential respect—a postmodern writer, inclined to discard the representation of character and moral predicaments as unwanted baggage. And I would like to claim that a writer is in most instances able to spin the sinew and flesh of mimetically persuasive character from the vital substance of his own life, however drastic the alchemical processes through which identity and sensibility and moral psychology are transmuted almost beyond recognition. The border, moreover, between control and spontaneous invention, between conscious thought and unconscious imagining, may often waver, even for a writer like Nabokov, and determining such boundaries is a futile exercise: what is crucial is that even in the midst of careful calculation, the life of the character draws from the quick of the writer's experience.

Let me begin with two autobiographical dates borrowed for events in *Pale Fire*, one quite consciously and the other perhaps not. In his fine analysis of the novel, Brian Boyd, in the only paragraph of strictly biographical criticism, the penultimate one of the chapter, notes that July 21, the day John Shade is cut down by an assassin's bullet, is the birthday of V. D. Nabokov, the writer's father. As Boyd goes on to observe, V. D. Nabokov was killed in Berlin in 1922 precisely as Shade is killed at the end of the novel, when his body intercepts a bullet aimed by a political terrorist at another man. This private calendric allusion to the most traumatic event of Nabokov's life is gratuitous to the artistic design of the novel but suggests the extent to which the imagining of the death of John Shade—and perhaps, as Boyd has argued, his actual survival of his own fictional demise—was a way of mastering the horror of his father's death. Shade, of course, is in no way a father figure for the author but more like an American alter ego. This is an identification to which we shall return.

Shade, the eminent poet and scholar of eighteenth-century literature, is Nabokov's coeval, born just a year later than his author (1900). Shade's unfortunate ugly-duckling daughter, Hazel, who commits suicide at the age of twenty-three, is born in 1934, the same year as Dmitri Nabokov, the author's only child. In terms of the workings of the plot, it would have made no difference whatever if Hazel had been born in 1933 or 1936. The choice of 1934, though it may reflect less deliberate calculation than the assassination date of July 21, points to a complicated emotional investment of Vladimir Nabokov in the invented life of John Shade. Of course, real Dmitri and fictional Hazel are in all respects, from gender to personal endowments, complete opposites: he, tall and good-looking, athletic and adventurous, a talented singer, a success with many women, a driver of fast sports cars; she, overweight and odd, without vocation, a hopeless wallflower. But if, as Shade tells Kinbote,

"Resemblances are the shadows of differences," there may be a way in the genesis of the novel in which differences are the shadows of resemblance. At the emotional heart of the poem "Pale Fire" is the death of the poet's daughter. The story of the two parents waiting by the television set on a windy, misty March night for the child who will never return is the most elaborately orchestrated piece of narrative in the Poem, and it is above all that wrenching loss which drives Shade's musings on what may lie beyond the opaque veil of earthly existence. Genetically, Hazel's death is a photographic negative developed from the anxiously guarded image of Dmitri's life. Nabokov, shaken as a young man by the violent loss of his father, had long pondered the dark possibility of losing a child as well, a fear explicitly embodied in the ghastly murder by fascist thugs of Adam Krug's only son in *Bend Sinister*. By 1961, when he was writing *Pale Fire*, this understandable free-floating anxiety had been given a specific gravity by the twenty-seven-year-old Dmitri's two favorite leisure activities: mountain climbing and racing sports cars. John Shade, the novelist's principal galley slave, lives out the anguish of a fate projected from the paternal fears of his master.

Nabokov has extrapolated, transmogrified, and redistributed bits and pieces of his inner life and personal circumstances in the characters of both Shade and Kinbote, so the play of antitheses and complementarity between poet and commentator is not only a thematic and structural game but also a vividly disguised vehicle of autobiographical exploration. Shade is the indigenous American counterpart to Nabokov the adoptive American writer, and a happily academic figure over against Nabokov's seventeen-year career as an amused, bemused, ambivalent—though grateful—transient in the groves of academe. Like Nabokov, he is a long-standing and contented monogamist and a successful writer confident of his own powers. He shares with his author a long list of pet peeves and preferences. Though he is a fictional construct with an invented biography, his poetry is, to all intents and purposes, the English poetry of Vladimir Nabokov in all its distinctive features— constrained, I would say, to recurrent moments of awkwardness by the mixed marriage of Popean couplets and twentieth-century colloquial English, but sometimes attaining a haunting eloquence compounded of witty verbal invention, precise observation of concrete particulars, and musical sound-play that is unmistakably Nabokovian, like this meditation on mortality and the possible afterworld:

> For we die every day; oblivion thrives
> Not on dry thighbones but on blood-ripe lives,
> And our best yesterdays are now foul piles
> Of crumpled names, phone numbers and foxed files.
> I'm ready to become a floweret
> Or a fat fly, but never, to forget.
> And I'll turn down eternity unless
> The melancholy and the tenderness
> Of moral life; the passion and the pain;
> The claret taillight of that dwindling plane
> Off Hesperus; your gesture of dismay
> On running out of cigarettes; the way
> You smile at dogs; the trail of silver slime
> Snails leave on flagstones; this good ink, this rhyme,
> This index card, this slender rubber band
> Which always forms, when dropped, an ampersand,
> Are found in Heaven by the newlydead
> Stored in its strongholds through the years. (lines
>   519–536)

Though a fictitious poet may be a poetic persona at two removes, it takes little effort to see here in the shadows of differences the underlying resemblance to Vladimir Nabokov composing in ink on file cards and affectionately addressing his own wife. The image of the rubber band as ampersand is one of many witty transformations of objects into printed symbols in the novel, and, together with the "lemniscate" traced by bicycle wheels and the figure eight it virtually represents (as in Iris Acht, mistress to King Charles's grandfather), it is an ideogram of the novel's structure: Poem flowing into Commentary and vice versa. That connection, not as a matter of formal structure but as an interplay of sensibilities, is also adumbrated here, perhaps not deliberately, in the single florid flourish—"The melancholy and the tenderness / . . . the passion and the pain"—in which the usually restrained Shade indulges, thus making momentary contact with the more flamboyant poetry of the melodramatic Kinbote's prose. There is one plangent moment in the Poem when the rooted American poet projects a beam of empathy onto the plight of a hopeless exile on the American landscape, thus replicating and refracting the process by which Nabokov, an exile happily rerooted in America for two decades, reconstitutes his own destiny in the novel in the opposed figures of the flourishing native poet and the hapless exiled king:

> Nor can one help the exile, the old man
> Dying in a motel, with the loud fan
> Revolving in the torrid prairie night
> And, from the outside, bits of colored light
> Reaching his bed like dark hands from the past
> Offering gems; and death is coming fast.
> He suffocates and conjures in two tongues
> The nebulae dilating in his lungs. (609–616)

It is hardly surprising that the self-obsessed commentator, coming across this rare instance in which the details of the Poem approximate the circumstances of his life, should read the passage as a literal prophecy of his last location in a motel in "Cedarn, Utana," writing his Commentary. In Kinbote's case, the shadow of difference between him and the novelist is dramatically long: he is a compulsively promiscuous homosexual, an anguished isolate, a guilt-ridden sinner clinging to a Dostoevskian belief in divine forgiveness, a foreigner who never gets America right (in this, a grotesquely tragic counterpart to the sadly comic Pnin), an intransigent vegetarian, and, of course, a deluded madman.

The one obvious link between Kinbote and Nabokov is figurative rather than psychological. Nabokov more than once likened his forced separation first from his native Russian cultural setting and then from the Russian language as his medium of artistic expression to the loss of throne and scepter. Although after the spectacular success of *Lolita* he came to "reign" on a global scale as one of the most celebrated writers of his age, Nabokov sometimes still reverted to the image of the literary kingdom he had been compelled to renounce on the brink of manhood, and in *Pale Fire* he constructed out of that image the governing fantasy of Charles Kinbote, who imagines himself to be the deposed monarch of Zembla and thrusts that plot into the foreground of the novel, repeatedly bemoaning the loss of Zemblan sunsets, the glitter of life in his capital city of Onhava, the melodious magic of his native poetry.

On reflection (obviously the right activity for this novel abounding in mirrors), Kinbote, for all his extravagance and perversity, exhibits many points of contact with his creator. He shares Nabokov's views on art and reality: "reality is neither the subject nor the object of true art, which creates its own special reality having nothing to do with the average 'reality' perceived by the communal eye" (p. 130). (The "communal eye," as we saw in Nabokov's letter to Khodasevich, is a pet peeve of VN's.) His judgment of violence and politics is identical with his author's: "The one who kills is always his victim's inferior" (p. 234). His wit is hard to distinguish from Nabokov's, as when he observes in a drawer of his rented house "an old but unused pocket diary optimistically maturing there until its calendric correspondencies came around again" (p. 84). Though Nabokov at times deliberately pushes Kinbote's language to flamboyant excesses in keeping with his extravagant character, as a stylist the mad commentator is often capable of truly Nabokovian lyricism and, even more frequently, of Nabokovian grotesque invention—"along [the underground ditch's] edge walked a sick bat like a cripple with a broken umbrella" (p. 133)—and of Nabokovian satiric humor, as in the Index entry for Thurgus the Third: "stout and bald, his nose like a congested plum, his martial mustache bristling with obsolete passion" (p. 314). Kinbote the fantast, master of the novel's prose, really eclipses the neo-Popean Shade as poet (and it makes no difference if one infers, as some critics a little improbably do, that Shade has invented Kinbote), and his declaration near the end is patently Nabokov's poetic credo: "I can do what only a true artist can do—pounce upon the forgotten butterfly of revelation, wean myself abruptly from the habit of things, see the web of the world, and the warp and the weft of that web" (p. 289). Note Nabokov's signature reference to butterflies here.

How does a figure so spectacularly different from its author end up speaking—resonantly if intermittently—in its author's voice? Fictional invention is usually a playing out by the writer of alternate lives, which quite often means—manifestly, I think, in Nabokov's case—a bringing to light of the buried underside of the writer's self. (This does not necessarily involve an

expression of the unconscious, Freudian or otherwise.) Nabokov's fondness for twisted protagonists (Kinbote is part of a
series that includes the nympholept Humbert Humbert and the
incestuous egoist Van Veen) is, among other things, a way of
camouflaging resemblance in obvious difference. As a writer so
absolutely committed to the autonomy of the imagination,
Nabokov was acutely conscious of the ways in which the imagination could distort the world, envelop a person in a solipsistic
bubble, impair the capacity for authentic intimate connection
with other people.

The obverse face of that fierce independence which was the
enabling condition of Nabokov's art was his living as a kind of
hidden isolate, for all the surface conviviality of his social be-
havior, sharing things deeply only with his wife. I don't mean to
suggest that he felt this as the dark fate of a *poète maudit*, but he
certainly used his novels to play out the drastic possibilities of
isolate imaginists exploiting humanity by using it as mere grist
for their imaginative mills. Sexual desire, because it so powerfully fuels the imagination in its most distortive operations, is
often the vehicle he chooses to create the isolated condition of
his protagonists.

Kinbote's troubled homosexuality is a case in point. Before
one leaps to the conclusion so often invoked in contemporary
America that the novel is "homophobic," one should note precisely what sort of homosexual Kinbote is represented to be. In
the formal design of the novel, his sexual identity is obviously
a neat antithesis to the happily heterosexual Shade, but it is its
moral implications that deserve special attention. He is, as I
have already noted, compulsively promiscuous, and he is also,
somewhat intermittently, a pedophile, two characteristics that
clearly do not obtain to most men drawn to the same sex as
objects of desire. (Whether psychologically his being in love
with John Shade is compatible with these two proclivities is a

question I am not competent to judge.) He cannot suppress the reflexive glimmer of lust for every pretty boy who enters his field of vision, even in the ultimate mountain motel room where he writes his Commentary and contemplates suicide. Since free-floating concupiscence, especially when its objects are adolescents, is a way of using people without much possibility of intimate connection except in the carnal sense, Kinbote is quite desperate in his isolation: "I cannot describe the depths of my loneliness and distress" (p. 95). His assertion of a certain resemblance between himself and Hazel Shade is not as mad as it might first seem (p. 193).

There are moral crimes perpetrated by a complete lack of imagination, and that is how Nabokov sees totalitarian terror. Its main representative in the novel is the assassin Jakob Gradus, the goon with the gun. But the artistic soul—see Gradus's anagrammatic reverse mirror image, "Sudarg of Bokay, a mirror maker of genius," as he is identified in the Index—is capable of perpetrating its own moral wrongs through excess of imagination. (Humbert Humbert is of course the prime instance of such perversity in Nabokov's fiction.) In Kinbote's fantasy life as Charles X of Zembla, the crucial focus of this sort of moral failing is his wife, Queen Disa. He has more than enough imagination to realize her suffering in their unconsummated marriage, to recognize that, against all reasonable odds, she loves him, and even to return her love, in a hypothetical way. But imagination becomes an instrument for reconciling himself to his unflagging neglect of her, even as he touches a certain tremulous chord of guilt, and she continues to languish in her abandonment, so she is perhaps more akin to Hazel Shade than he is. The passage I have quoted in the preceding essay on *Pale Fire* is worth recalling here:

He dreamed of her more often, and with incomparably more poignancy, than his surface-life warranted; these dreams occurred when he least thought of her, and worries in no way connected with her assumed her image in the subliminal world as a battle or a reform becomes a bird of wonder in a tale for children. These heartrending dreams transformed the drab prose of his feelings for her into strong and strange poetry, subsiding undulations of which would flash and disturb him throughout the day, bringing back the pang and the richness—and then only the pang, and then only its glancing reflection—but not affecting at all his attitude toward Disa. (p. 209)

At moments like this—and there are many of them in the novel—the narrator is not merely a grotesquely carved wooden king in a literary game of chess, but speaks through his own predicament to a moral question over which the author has surely brooded. Without imagination, life can scarcely be thought of as human. But that very faculty, which provides our keenest gratification in experiencing love, art, and the natural world, can be used to bend all things violently into its own shape (Humbert vis-à-vis Lolita, Kinbote vis-à-vis Shade and his Poem); alternately, it can offer the sweet substitute of its own seductive rhythms instead of engagement with another human life (Kinbote vis-à-vis Disa). In the representation of the passage just quoted of Charles's sad dreams about Disa, Nabokov cunningly introduces the novel's recurrent motif of undulating reflections, but here the flashing reflections give us the image of an inner life turned into an endless hall of mirrors never leading to the outside.

As a fictional character, Kinbote represents a rare balancing act. In some ways, of course, he is a figure of fun: inveterate bumbler, self-made misfit, shameless egotist, incorrigible pedant. But his suffering is finally no joke, even when Nabokov has him describe it in patently lurid terms. In fact, much of the language Nabokov fashions to express Kinbote's anguish is, without parody or camp, an evocative articulation of what it is like to be a splendid master of imagination, steeped in its flood of intensities but carried off from the sustaining connections of human commonality. Is it possible that through this utterly different figure Nabokov is probing the dark underside of his own vocation as a novelist inventing worlds?

Kinbote the tormented theist can at some moments speak in one voice with Nabokov the happy metaphysical nontheist, not only in an artistic credo but in a philosophic credo as well. Novelist and protagonist clearly converge in this ringing affirmation by Kinbote of what God is not: "He is not despair. He is not terror. He is not the earth rattling in one's throat, not the black hum in one's ears fading to nothing in nothing. I know also that the world could not have occurred fortuitously and that somehow Mind is involved as a main factor in the making of the universe" (p. 227). Kinbote and Shade and Nabokov come together in this declaration of faith. *Pale Fire* was composed not only out of its author's exuberant delight in his own architectonic and inventive skills but also out of his deepest troubled reflections on mortality, the threat of modern political violence and the sheer randomness of destruction, and the dangers of living too much through the imagination. The oddly paired destinies he imagines in Kinbote and Shade, together with the intricate artifice through which they are represented, reach toward a serious visionary glimpse of order behind seeming arbitrary chaos, pattern implicit even in what looks like random destruction, and a luminous prospect beyond the feared blackness of nothing fading into nothing. In these respects, the two fictional figures are flesh of his flesh.

6

Ada, or the Perils of Paradise

Ada occupies a problematically dominant place among Nabokov's novels. Twice as long as any other work of fiction he wrote, this ambitious, formally elaborate, fantastically inventive novel published in his seventieth year was clearly intended as a culmination of the distinctive artistic enterprise to which he devoted half a century. In it he sought to incorporate and reach beyond the achievement of his two English masterpieces, *Lolita* and *Pale Fire* (both of which are abundantly alluded to in *Ada*). Or, to invoke a painterly analogy specifically brought to our attention several times in the novel, *Ada* is the third panel in a Boschean triptych, a novelistic Garden of Earthly Delights that began with *Lolita* in 1954, in which there is a paradoxical fusion of lyricism and the grotesque, of free-wheeling invention and scrupulous attention to familiar reality, in which beauty flowers from perversion, a radiant dream of happiness from the shadow of loneliness and exile.

Lolita had been the most brilliant in the line of books that since the 1920s had studied the vertiginous intercrossings of imagination and reality, the artist and his world, through athletically allusive, involuted, and parodic forms. These same concerns were then given even more intricate formal expression in

Pale Fire as the new central emphasis in *Lolita* on the quest for a paradisiac past (Humbert Humbert's golden "princedom by the sea") appeared in oblique refraction through Kinbote's longing for his lost kingdom. In *Ada*, as we shall see in detail, Nabokov moved boldly from a vision of paradise lost to one of paradise regained—or retained—for the first time in his fiction, though following the precedent of the autobiographical *Speak, Memory*; and he also produced the most capaciously encompassing of all his parodic forms.

The result of this consciously culminating effort was, of course, greeted with catcalls by certain readers as a supreme monstrosity of literary narcissism, and hailed with jubilation by Nabokov loyalists as a climactic masterpiece. Rereading *Ada* years after its publication, I find it a dazzling, but at times also exasperating, near-masterpiece that lacks the perfect selectivity and control of *Lolita* and *Pale Fire*. At the book's weaker moments, one feels that the novelist permits himself too much, inadvertently unraveling threads in his own rich tapestry through his eagerness to pursue every linguistic quibble, every gratuitous turn of a sexual or literary double meaning. In this last major work, Nabokov invented a hypothetical antiworld where everything culturally precious to him—the Russian, English, and French languages, the vanished graces of his parents' aristocratic estate—could be harmoniously combined; and it may be that this embarrassment of riches encouraged a certain softness, made it more difficult for him to distinguish between imaginative necessity and private indulgence. But these recurrent capitulations to the temptations of mere byplay are the defect of a virtue; for the exuberance of the novel's more meaningful playfulness in fact brings it close to the crowning achievement Nabokov sought. Through many extraordinary passages, and in its larger design, *Ada* succeeds in illuminating in new

depth and breadth the relation between art, reality, and the evanescent ever-never presence of time past; and it is that illumination which chiefly deserves our attention.

The dimension of parody, established with the first words of
the text, has to be kept clearly in perspective, for nowhere else
in Nabokov's writing is the parodic mode made so pervasive
and so deliberately obtrusive as here. Because parody is intrinsic to Nabokov's method, and because he more often parodies
plot, situation, and motif than style and narrative technique, a
plot-summary of any of his novels is bound to be thoroughly
misleading, but perhaps more so for *Ada* than for any other
work. (To mislead the unsuspecting, of course, is precisely what
he always intends: thus, the four concluding paragraphs of *Ada*
are a pitchman's synopsis of the book, the prose of the novel
followed by what the narrator, tongue in cheek, calls "the poetry
of its blurb.") *Ada*—which, when it is going well, manages to be
one of the sunniest works of fiction written in the twentieth
century—sounds, to judge by the bare outlines of its plot, like
a dark drama of fatal, incestuous passion.

Van Veen, the retrospective nonagenarian narrator, has an
ecstatic affair at the age of fourteen with twelve-year-old Ada,
ostensibly his cousin, later discovered to be his sister. The two
are irresistibly drawn to each other by their inner natures but
are separated by social taboo and the course of outward events.
In the two decades from early adolescence to mature adulthood, the lovers enjoy four fleeting periods of illicit ardor together, but each time the subsequent separation is longer; and,
while Van seeks the simulacrum of his Ada in a thousand
whores and mistresses, both he and she are physically thick-
ened and coarsened by the passing years, until at last they come
together in late middle age, all passion not spent but certainly
muted. In the background, moreover, of their partings and

joinings, as the third, unequal angle of a thoroughly incestuous triangle, is the pathetic figure of Lucette, their mutual half-sister, who loves Van relentlessly body and soul, loves Ada, periodically, in a more strictly bodily sense, and finally destroys herself when she is rejected by Van.

All this may sound like rather lurid stuff, especially when one adds that there is a much higher degree of descriptive specification about sexual matters here than anywhere else in Nabokov's fiction. And it must be conceded that there are moments when the writer's sense of freedom in treating sexual materials leads to a certain gloating tone—most evidently, in the repeated evocation of an international network of elite whorehouses to which Van Veen becomes habituated.

In any case, the actual tenor of the novel as a whole is, of course, precisely the opposite of what this summary suggests. On a stylistic level, the seeming paradox is easy enough to explain: Nabokov's intricately wrought, elaborately figurative style, with its painterly effects and its perspectivist mirror-games, transmutes objects of description, even the most pungently physical objects, into magical *objets d'art*. When, for example, the narrator, in a spectacular set piece, describes all three siblings in bed together (surely a parody of the *ménage à trois* grapplings that are stock scenes of pornographic literature), he invites us to view the action as though it were reflected in the ceiling mirror of a fancy brothel, and then proceeds to convert the rampant eroticism into a formal contrasting and blending of colors and movements. Physical details are not spared—"the detail is all," Van Veen had affirmed earlier about the reality of all experience and memory; but, to cite a strategic instance, the exposed sexual fluff of redheaded Lucette and black-haired Ada becomes here a new-fledged firebird and an enchanting raven, varicolored birds of paradise in a poet's Wonderland.

Nabokov has often been celebrated for his brilliance as a stylist. Yet it is important to recognize that this brilliance, perhaps most centrally in *Ada*, is not ornamental, as in some of his American imitators, but the necessary instrument of a serious ontological enterprise: to rescue reality from the bland nonentity of stereotypicality and from the terrifying rush of mortality by reshaping objects, relations, existential states, through the power of metaphor and wit, so that they become endowed with an arresting life of their own. An incidental samovar observed in passing "expressed fragments of its surroundings in demented fantasies of a primitive genre."[1] (This in fact sounds a bit like Dickens.) Lucette drowning sees her existence dissolve in a receding series of selves and perceives that "what death amounted to was only a more complete assortment of the infinite fractions of solitude" (p. 494). Van Veen, driving through the Alps to his first rendezvous with Ada after a separation of fifteen years, sees from his flesh (to borrow an apposite idiom from Job) the palpable reality of time as his recent telephone conversation with Ada and his view of the landscape around him are transformed in the alembic of consciousness into a summarizing metaphor:

> That telephone voice, by resurrecting the past and linking it up with the present, with the darkening slate-blue mountains beyond the lake, with the spangles of the sun wake dancing through the poplars, formed the centerpiece in his deepest perception of tangible time, the glittering "now" that was the only reality of Time's texture. (p. 556)

As a vivid commentary on what he aspires to achieve through style, Nabokov likens the youthful Van's astonishing agility in walking on his hands to the function of metaphor in Van's later work as a writer:

> It was the standing of a metaphor on its head not for the sake of the trick's difficulty, but in order to perceive an ascending waterfall or a sunrise in reverse: a triumph, in a sense, over the ardis of time. . . . Van on the stage was performing organically what his figures of speech were to perform later in life—acrobatic wonders that had never been expected from them and which frightened children. (p. 185)

We shall devote further attention later to those acrobatic wonders when we consider Nabokov's rendering of Ada and the paradisiac world of youth with which she is inextricably associated.

When one moves from effects of style to the larger narrative patterns of the novel, it is difficult to make full sense of the incestuous complications without attention to the ubiquitous use of literary allusion. In order to talk about the allusions, something first must be said about the setting. The principal action of *Ada* takes place, one recalls, in the late nineteenth and early twentieth centuries of a world alternately referred to as Antiterra and Daemonia, which has the same geography as our world but a teasingly different though parallel history. The area we call Russia having been conquered some centuries earlier by the Tartars, America has been settled by Russian as well as English and French colonists; and so Nabokov's own three native languages and literary traditions are able to flourish side by side, as complementary parts of a single national culture. From a terrestrial viewpoint—Terra the Fair, by the way, is a supposedly celestial place believed in mainly by the deranged on Antiterra—periods as well as cultural boundaries have been hybridized; the daemonian nineteenth century combines the quiet country houses of Chekhov and Jane Austen with telephones, airplanes, skyscrapers; a mock-Maupassant figure is contemporaneous with the author of a *Lolita*-like novel masquerading (anagrammatically) as J. L. Borges.

This device of a fictional antiworld gives Nabokov a free hand to combine and permute the materials of culture and history in piquant and suggestive ways, though perhaps, as I have already proposed, it also sometimes tempts him into self-indulgence; so that one begins to feel he is playing his games of anagrams, trilingual puns, coded hints, and conflated allusions for their own sake, not because they have any imaginative necessity in a larger design. Vladimir Nabokov, that is, at times rather too closely resembles his anagrammatic double in the novel, Baron Klim Avidov, bequeathing ornate sets of super-Scrabble to the characters and, implicitly, to the readers.

It must be admitted, though, that some of the incidental games, especially those involving literary figures, are amusing enough in themselves that one would hesitate to give them up. My own favorite is the treatment of T. S. Eliot, who appears as a truncated version of his own ape-necked Sweeney, "solemn Kithar Sween, a banker who at sixty-five had become an avant-garde author; . . . had produced *The Waistline*, a satire in free verse on Anglo-American feeding habits" (pp. 505–506); and who is seen, in most poetic justice for a versifier of anti-Semitic innuendoes, in the company of "old Eliot," a Jewish real-estate man.

The most important advantage, in any case, that Nabokov gains through the freedom he allows himself to shuttle across temporal and cultural boundaries is that he is able to compress into the life space of his protagonist a parodic review of the development of the novel. The story begins in the classic age of the novel, and everything that happens, really, occurs in purely novelistic time and novelistic space. Ardis Manor, where young Van Veen will meet Ada, is glimpsed for the first time, characteristically, in the following fashion: "At the next turning, the romantic mansion appeared on the gentle eminence of old novels" (p. 35). The narrative is frequently punctuated with such notations to remind us that everything is taking place against a ground of familiar and perhaps jaded literary conventions, as the view shifts quickly, and not necessarily chronologically, from Romantic *récit* to Jane Austen, Turgenev, Dickens, Flaubert, Aksakov, Dostoevsky, the pornographic novel, the gothic novel, Joyce, and Nabokov beyond them. The "plot," in fact, is from one point of view composed of a string of stock scenes from the traditional novel: the young man's return to the ancestral manor; the festive picnic; the formal dinner; a midnight conflagration on the old estate; the distraught hero's flight at dawn from hearth and home as the result of a misunderstanding; the duel; the hero's profligacy in the great metropolis, and so forth.

Though the technique of allusion is common to all Nabokov's novels, there is a special thematic justification for this recapitulation in parody of the history of a genre; for what Van Veen's story represents is a reversal of the major thematic movement of the novel as a genre. The novel characteristically has concerned itself with lost illusions—the phrase, of course, was used as a title by Balzac in a central work—from the quixotic knight who finally abandons his pursuit of a golden age, a broken man renouncing his chivalric enterprise and dying, to Flaubert's Emma, spitting out her daydreams of a blue beyond in the last hideous retches of an arsenic suicide; to Anna Karenina— the first sentence of her story is quoted, in reverse, in the first sentence of *Ada*—ending her tortured love under the wheels of a locomotive. What "happy endings" one finds in the classic novel are generally a matter of mere acquiescence to convention

(Dickens) or sober accommodation of the protagonists to society (Jane Austen, George Eliot). *Ada*, in direct contrast, is an attempt to return to paradise, to establish, in fact, the luminous vision of youth and love's first fulfillment as the most intensely, perdurably real experience we know. It bears affinities both with Molly Bloom's great lyric recall of her first flowering of love at the end of *Ulysses* and with Proust's triumph over time through art in the last volume of his novel, but it is a more concerted frontal attack on Eden than either.

Two key allusions are especially helpful in understanding what Nabokov is up to with his incestuous lovers. One is simple, a mere negative parallel to serve as a foil; the other is complex, being a kind of imaginative model for the whole book and ramifying into other related allusions. Several passing references are made to Chateaubriand: Ada jokingly calls Van her "René"; and the first half of the novel's title, *Ada, or Ardor*, looks suspiciously like a parody of that most Romantic title, *René ou les effets des passions*. René, like Van, is a singular man with an artist's soul who enjoys the rare delights of bucolic ambles with his dear sister until the incestuous nature of her attachment to him forces them to separate. So much for the parallels; all the rest is pointed contrast.

René is a book suffused with Romantic *mal du siècle*; and René and Amélie, unlike the Veen siblings, are anything but "children of Venus." The parodic fulfillment of premoral desire is quite unthinkable for René and his sister, so that the very existence of such desire drives Amélie into a convent and ultimately leads to martyrs' deaths for both of them. In *Ada*, one can see from the sunlit River Ladore near the Ardis estate a view of Bryant's Castle (gallicized, Chateaubriand), "remote and romantically black on its oak-timbered hill" (p. 215). The chief quality of Van Veen's world, by contrast, is brightness and intimate closeness, social and sexual, tactile and visual; and its oak trees, as we shall see, are part of a landscape very different from the dark romantic wood. René actively longs for death, even before the revelation of his sister's passion; he sees in it a hazy, alluring *ailleurs*, as though the concrete objects of this world could not conceivably satisfy the needs of his own swoon of infinite desire. Nabokov's hero and heroine, on the other hand, delight in the concrete particulars of this world—Ada is a naturalist, Van an artist—observe and recall them with tender, meticulous care; and they both passionately love existence in this world, each being the other's ultimate point of anchorage in it, Van's male V or arrowhead (*ardis* in Greek) perfectly fitting into its inverted and crossed female mirror image, the A of his sister-soul (ideogrammatists take note, Freudians beware). The mirror play of Van's and Ada's initials—underscored at one point when Nabokov finds dramatic occasion to print the A upside down—suggests that the two are perfect lovers because ultimately they are complementary halves of one self. Indeed, Van's book is really "written" by the two of them, one imagination called "Vaniada" expressing itself in two antiphonal voices. The birthmark on the back of Van's right hand reappears in exactly the corresponding spot on Ada's left hand, for both physically and psychically the lovers are really the two halves of that androgynous pristine human zestfully described by Aristophanes in Plato's *Symposium* and at one point explicitly alluded to by Nabokov.

According to rabbinic legend, Adam in the garden before the creation of Eve was androgynous; and it is clear that Nabokov, like the rabbis, has conjoined the Greek and Hebrew myths, creating in his deliciously intertwined sister and brother an image of prelapsarian, unfragmented humanity.

A major clue to Nabokov's intention in this respect is the repeated allusion, especially in the Ardis section of the novel, to one of the most splendidly realized experiences of paradise in English poetry, Andrew Marvell's "The Garden." Adolescent Ada tries to translate the poem into French—in her version, an oak tree stands prominently at the beginning of the second line; after the lovers' first separation, the poem, most appropriately, serves as a code-key for the letters in cipher that they exchange. (The other code-key is Rimbaud's *Mémoire*, another ripely sensual poem of bucolic repose, rich in color imagery, presided over by "the gambol of angels.") The second stanza of Marvell's poem, not quoted in the novel, begins as follows: "Fair quiet, have I found thee here, / And Innocence thy Sister dear! / Mistaken long, I sought you then / In busie Companies of Men." The lines are, of course, applicable point for point to the novel, a kind of adumbration of its plot, though both "sister" and "innocence" are given rather different meanings. Marvell's poem is a vision of bliss beyond the raging of physical passion. The solitary garden-dweller, however, does revel in the pleasures of the senses, luscious fruit dropping from the trees to delight his palate, while his mind withdraws into the happiness of self-contemplation where it—like the author of *Ada*?—"creates, transcending these, / Far other Worlds, and other Seas." In *Ada*'s ardisiac setting, luscious fruit also comes falling from the branches, when the tree-climbing young Ada slips and ends up straddling an astonished Van from the front, thus offering him an unexpectedly intimate first kiss. In a moment Ada will claim that this is the Tree of Knowledge, brought to the Ardis estate from Eden, a national park, but her slip from its branches clearly enacts a Happy Fall; for in this garden, as in Marvell's, no fatal sin is really possible. Marvell's poem also gives us a comic image of a fall with no evil consequences: "Stumbling on Melons, as I pass, / Insnar'd with Flow'rs, I fall on Grass." The interlaced limbs of ardently tumbling Van and Ada are similarly assimilated to the premoral world of vegetation, likened to tendril climbers; and Van, rushing away from a last embrace of Ada at the moment of their first separation, is actually described as "stumbling on melons," an allusion that would seem to promise that he will eventually return to his Ada-Ardis-Eden. It is the concluding stanza, however, of Marvell's "The Garden" that offers the most suggestive model for what Nabokov seeks to achieve in *Ada*. After the garden-dweller's soul, whetting and combing its silver wings among the branches, has experienced ecstasy, the poet glances backward at the first Adam's paradise, then returns us to the "real" world of time; but it is time now transfigured by art, nature ordered by "the skillful Gardener" in a floral sundial to measure time. The industrious bee, then, no less than man, "computes its time" (in seventeenth-century pronunciation as in ours, a pun on "thyme" and thus a truly Nabokovian wordplay) with herbs and flowers; time the eroder has been alchemized in this artful re-creation of paradise into a golden translucence, delighting palate and eye. Nabokov means to create just such an interinvolvement of art and pleasure transcending time, or rather capturing its elusive living "texture," as Van Veen calls it; and this, finally, is the dramatic function of the novel's unflagging emphasis on erotic experience.

The point is made clearer in the novel by yet another allusion. Marvell's "The Garden" modulates into several other poems in the course of the narrative, but the most significant is Baudelaire's "*Invitation au voyage*," which is burlesqued in the novel with an oak tree inserted in the second and third line, to establish the cross-link with Marvell. Baudelaire's poem is also a ravishing dream of a perfect world, a world saturated with both generally sensual and specifically erotic delight, but realized, as such bliss can only be realized, through the beautiful ordering of art. Against the background of the novel, the famous opening lines of the poem become an evocation of Ardis, Van addressing Ada: *"Mon enfant, ma soeur, / Songe à la douceur / D'aller là-bas vivre ensemble! / Aimer à loisir / Aimer et mourir / Au pays qui te ressemble"* (My child, my sister, / imagine the sweetness / of going there to live together! / To love in leisure / to love and die / in the land that is like you). It is noteworthy that fragments of these lines are bandied about by Ada at the point in the narrative when their first sexual intimacy is recollected; significantly, this is the one moment in the novel when Ada actually says to Van that they are not two different people.

Baudelaire's poem, then, suggests what is also clear in the novel in other ways: that *Ada* is formed on the paradox of rendering the perfect state of nature through a perfect state of art, self-conscious and exquisitely ordered. In this respect, Nabokov also follows the model of Milton (who is burlesqued in tetrameters at one point) in the fourth book of *Paradise Lost*, where prelapsarian Eden is described through the most finely ostentatious artifice—a natural garden full of sapphire founts, sands of gold, burnished fruit, crystal-mirror brooks, in which the preceding literary tradition of envisioned paradises is incorporated through the cunning strategy of negation ("Not that fair field / Of Enna" and so forth). It may be that *Ada* pays a price as a novel for being an extended poetic vision of Eden: Van and Ada sometimes seem to be more voices and images in a lyric poem than novelistic characters; the excess of formal perfection they must sustain makes them less interesting individually, less humanly engaging, than many of Nabokov's previous protagonists. In compensation, the expression in *Ada* of a lover's consummated delight in life and beauty is an achievement that has few equals in the history of the novel. Here is one brief but representative and thematically central instance, in which the lovers' present is juxtaposed with their ardisiac past:

> Her plump, stickily glistening lips smiled.
> (When I kiss you here, he said to her years later, I always remember that blue morning on the balcony when you were eating a *tartine au miel*; so much better in French.)
> The classical beauty of clover honey, smooth, pale, translucent, freely flowing from the spoon and soaking my love's bread and butter in liquid brass. The crumb steeped in nectar. (p. 75)

The honeyed slice of bread here is very much a Nabokovian equivalent of Proust's *petite madeleine* and, especially, of that more erotic tidbit, the ambrosial seedcake Molly Bloom puts from her mouth into her young lover Leopold's. Through its sweetness, past and present fuse; or, to speak more precisely, they fuse through its sweetness minutely observed and recollected, then distilled into the lucid order of a prose poem that moves in alliterative music through a poised choreography of dactyls and trochees to the culminating metaphorical paradox of the honey as liquid brass and the final substitution of nectar for the honey, now become "literally" food for the gods.

It is really for the experience of such moments—and there are many of them in the course of the novel—that *Ada* exists. To state this in generic terms, *Ada* is, in a rather precise sense of the word, Nabokov's most lyric novel. Characterization, certainly when compared with his own earlier fiction, tends to be abstract or schematic; and the operation of plot, always a source of fascination for Nabokov the ingenious craftsman, is somewhat problematic here, especially in the long, telescoped period after Van's and Ada's youth. This is a novel about time, Van Veen repeatedly reminds us, which means that it is a novel about memory, a faculty that in Nabokov's view can serve us vitally only if we exercise the finest, fullest attentiveness to the life of each moment and, ideally, also the control of language required to focus the moment recalled. Nearly halfway through the novel, one character is described trying "to *realize* (in the rare full sense of the word), . . . to *possess* the reality of a fact by forcing it into the sensuous center" (p. 251); and a page later, the narrator, with continuing italic emphasis, goes on to say that such realization can be effected only through "that *third sight* (individual, magically detailed imagination) which many otherwise ordinary and conformant people may also possess, but without which memory (even that of a profound 'thinker' or technician of genius) is, let us face it, a stereotype or a tearsheet." *Ada* is a series of verbal experiments in making one *realize* in the rare full sense of the word. If a reader fails to see that, there is scarcely any point in reading the book at all; once attuned to this central purpose, the reader may find ample compensation for all the incidental flaws.

In order to understand more concretely how this process of realization works in the novel, let us consider two further images of young Ada recalled (by her lover, of course, almost eight decades after the fact) to set alongside the moment of the *tartine au miel* we have already observed. Van remembers watching Ada during an evening game of "Flavita" (Baron Klim Avidov's super-Scrabble) in the halcyon year of 1884:

> The bloom streaking Ada's arm, the pale blue of the veins in its hollow, the charred-wood odor of her hair shining brownly next to the lampshade's parchment (a translucent

lakescape with Japanese dragons), scored infinitely more points than those tensed fingers bunched on the pencil stub could ever add up in the past, present or future. (p. 218)

This is beautiful, and it is also wittily complicated in a peculiarly satisfying way. The verbal portraitist is attentive to the fine modulations of color, texture, and odor in his subject, with the oddly adverbial "shining brownly" intimating the suggestively kinetic sense of hue that a gifted colorist can produce in a subtle composition. (Ada's hair is actually black, but Nabokov is aware of the way colors assume different values when orchestrated together and depending on the source of the light.) Thus, through individual, magically detailed imagination, Ada at the game table, otherwise elusive as all objects of memory are elusive, is forced into the sensuous center. What she means to the imagination of her enraptured beholder infinitely transcends the arithmetic scores of the anagrammatic game they have been playing; and the reference to past, present, and future is strategically important, because Ada as a luminous image treasured in the memory of the artist becomes an eternal present, beyond the ravages of time, and serves as the fulfilled quest of the novel as a whole. This evocation of Ada is not only artful, but, like most of what happens in the novel, it is set against another artwork: the translucent lakescape of the parchment lampshade with its Japanese dragons. The most immediate function of this detail is to contribute to the scenic realization of the moment, but it is also, like so many other artworks that Nabokov introduces, an analogue and an inverted reflection of the world of the novel. The lampshade painting is executed, one assumes, with reticent Oriental brushstrokes, quite unlike the Boschean descriptive vividness of the novel's technique. Instead of the serpents of Ada's Eden, there are Japanese dragons; instead of Ardis's rural streams, a lake.

A more elaborate instance of Ada's being set off against serpentine art occurs earlier in the novel, when she is a still virginal, though already distinctly nubile, twelve-year-old:

> His sentimental education now went fast. Next morning, he happened to catch sight of her washing her face and arms over an old-fashioned basin on a rococo stand, her hair knotted on the top of her head, her nightgown twisted around her waist like a clumsy corolla out of which issued her slim back, rib-shaded on the near side. A fat snake of porcelain curled around the basin, and as both the reptile and he stopped to watch Eve and the soft woggle of her bud-breasts in profile, a big mulberry-colored cake of soap slithered out of her hand, and her black-socked foot hooked the door shut with a bang which was more the echo of the soap's crashing against the marble board than a sign of pudic displeasure. (p. 60)

As in the scene of Ada by the lamp, painterly attention is given to shading and color, with that wonderful mulberry-colored soap somehow bringing the whole scene into bright focus and, at the same time, introducing a delicate suggestion of gustatory delight (the berries) into the vision of soapy Ada in her ritual of ablution. But, where Ada at the game table was a static portrait, movement dominates this passage, from the scrubbing hands of the beginning through the soft woggle of the small breasts in the middle to the door kicked shut at the end. Indeed, even what should logically be static begins strangely to move. Ada's slim back "issues" from her pulled-down nightgown like an object in fluid motion, and the "nightgown twisted" is a noun with a participle ambiguously turning itself into an active verb, so that the "clumsy corolla" of the garment can provide a perfect compositional parallel, in floral imagery, to the fat porcelain snake curling around the basin. The snake's movement is then imparted to the bar of soap, which "slithers" out of Ada's hand. The rococo serpent, of course, an item of aristocratic bric-à-brac, is permanently frozen as a piece of decorative sculpture but seems to possess (or to have possessed) movement, it being in the nature of plastic art to create the illusion of kinesis out of perfect stasis. The enamored Van, then, can wittily recruit the snake as a fellow admirer of Ada's beauty, imagining that the reptile observer like himself has momentarily stopped in its tracks with amazement over what it beholds. A snake observing a lovely girl obviously points back to that forever fateful moment at the beginning of Genesis, but this fat fellow seems more a jovial attendant to the girl's loveliness than a sinister seducer. The question of where or whether evil enters the Veens' Eden, a place paradoxically rich in demonic nomenclature, is not easy to resolve; and we shall try to sort out some of the main elements of that issue in a moment.

First, however, I should like to point out how traditional this whole enterprise of realizing experience is, at least in one crucial respect. For the moments Van Veen re-creates for us are not taken from indifferent topics. Almost all the truly memorable ones, like the three we have just considered, are sensuous meditations on the image of Ada. If he and she are two halves of a primal self, there is complementarity rather than equality between them, because he is the artist, she the subject, model, muse. Nabokov had at first thought of calling the novel *The Texture of Time*, a title he then relegated to a metaphysical work by Van Veen, but his book had to be called *Ada* for the same reason that the sundry sonnet cycles of the English Renaissance were emblazoned with titles like Delia, Diana, Phyllis, Celia. Art, to borrow the vocabulary of the "Viennese quack" Nabokov never tired of mocking, is a flow of libidinous energy toward the world, a formally coherent reenactment—perhaps more intensification than compensation—of the pleasure the artist has known in the world. And for the male-dominated Western tradition, at least as far back as Dante, the emblem, talisman, or goal of this pleasure is the figure of a beloved woman; it is through her that the artist comes to realize the fullness of life. "He saw reflected in her," Van says of himself and Ada just before the end, "everything that his fastidious and fierce spirit sought in life" (p. 574).

Nabokov had played with this tradition once before in his other English novel bearing a woman's name as title, but Lolita is, of course, in many respects a highly ironic version of the myth of the Muse or Eternal Beloved, shrewdly raising all sorts of psychological, moral, and epistemological questions about what is involved in a man's addiction to such a myth. Ada, less novelistic and more lyric than its predecessor, attempts to renew the myth without ironic subversion, which may explain some of its weaknesses but is also the reason for its distinctive beauty. At one point, Van is unsettled to learn that his love for Ada has become the subject among the inhabitants of the Ardis region of a whole cycle of romances, epics, folk songs, ballads sung to the strum of seven-stringed Russian lyres. His own task is to present a more scrupulous version that will not falsify the sensuous truth of his lifelong love, in a literary art that is by turns lyrical, painterly, wittily playful, scientific, aphoristic, self-reflective. The result of this effort will be the "real" Ada, and a 589-page poem called Ada.

All this still leaves unexplained the lurking elements of shadow in Nabokov's large, sunny picture. At several points in the novel the narrator takes pains to inform us that Ada is the genitive form of the Russian word for hell. This makes Ada an exact etymological antithesis of the Renaissance poet's fair beloved, Celia, a name formed from the Latin for heaven. The main point, I would assume, is that Ada and Van in their Eden are in a state before the knowledge of good and evil, when heaven and hell cannot be distinguished. This also suggests, however, that there could be an ambiguous underside of evil in the Edenic fulfillment offered Van by his sister-soul, and the suicide to which the two of them inadvertently drive Lucette may indicate that a paradisiac love can have evil consequences when it impinges on the lives of others outside the garden; that there may be something essentially destructive in a passion that is so relentlessly an *égoïsme à deux*. An oddly grim fatality accompanies the long history of Ada's and Van's raptures. All four of their putative and actual parents come to a bad end, two of them being quite mad at the end, and one of them, Dan Veen, actually dying an odd Boschean death under the delusion that he is being ridden by a large rodent, a detail he remembers from Bosch's *The Garden of Earthly Delights*. Nabokov's invocation of that painting as one possible model for his project in *Ada* is itself an indication that his notion of Eden has its darker aspects. Bosch is praised by Demon Veen for the sheer freedom he exercised, "enjoying himself by crossbreeding casual fancies just for the fun of the contour, . . . the exquisite surprise of the unusual orifice" (p. 417), and Nabokov means to emulate that uninhibited exuberance of invention in his novel. But *The Garden of Earthly Delights* is not merely, as Demon Veen contends, an expression of the artist's delight in freely manipulating the medium; it is also a disturbingly ambiguous conception of the terrestrial paradise. Its central panel, "In Praise of Lust," is a panoramic representation of polymorphous perversity in which the actors look more often like doomed souls than gleeful sybarites. The right panel of the triptych, moreover, is no garden at all, but a vision of damnation against a black background, crowded with the usual Boschean monsters and eerie images of dismemberment, and entitled, because of the musical instruments in the foreground, "Musical Hell."

Did Nabokov mean to suggest that there is something ultimately monstrous about the artistic imagination itself; that, given absolute freedom, it will conjure up not only beautiful birds of paradise but the most fearful monstrosities as well—as Humbert Humbert so memorably illustrates? Here, as in other respects, there might be a moment of convergence between Nabokov's view of the mind and Freud's, however great the polemic distance that the novelist interposed between himself and psychoanalysis. Van Veen may even be intended, as Ellen Pifer has argued in a book about the moral dimension of Nabokov's fiction,[2] as another in the series of manipulative, sinister artist-figures that goes back to Axel Rex in *Laughter in the Dark*. There is something distinctly chilling about Van Veen's relation to everyone and everything except Ada and his own writing. Beyond the perimeter of his private garden-world and his literary lucubrations, he is a snob, a cold sensualist, and even on occasion a violent brute (as when he blinds the blackmailer Kim by caning him across the eyes). But if it was Nabokov's intention somehow to expose Van Veen, it is an intention not held in steady focus; for it is clear that the author shares many aspects of Van's sensibility and imaginatively participates in Van's dearest artistic and metaphysical aspirations, inviting us as readers to do so as well. The perilous closeness of beauty and monstrosity is manifestly an idea Nabokov conjures in this most ambitious, and most avowedly Boschean, of his novels, but it remains uncertain whether he actually succeeded in

defining the relationship between those antitheses in fictionally cogent terms.

In any event, the ultimate sense that the novel means to project is of all threats of evil, including the evil of the corrosive
passage of time, finally transcended by the twinned power of art
and love. One last clue encodes this idea as a signature of affirmation at the end of the novel. Moving around mysteriously in
the background of the concluding section is an unexplained
figure named Ronald Oranger. Since he marries the typist responsible for Van's manuscript, and since he and his wife, according to a prefatory note, are the only significant persons
mentioned in the book still alive when it is published, one may
assume that his is the final responsibility for the text of *Ada*, and
that he is the presiding spirit at the end. All we really know
about him is his name, which, of course, means "orange tree" in
French. No orange trees are explicitly mentioned in Marvell's
"The Garden," though they are spectacularly present in "Ber-
mudas," another remarkable poem by Marvell about a garden-
paradise. In any case, "Ronald Oranger" in a Nabokov novel has
a suspiciously anagrammatic look, and could well be rearranged
as a reversal of the book's title, "angel nor ardor"—which is to
say that the fixative force of art, working through the imagination of love, has extracted heaven from hell, Eden from Ada,
and established a perfected state that originates in the carnal
passions but goes quite beyond them.

If in fact such an anagrammatic code was intended by Nabokov, one could justifiably dismiss it as the gesture of a writer
who had spent too much time playing Scrabble. Fortunately,
the code-games and allusions in *Ada* are merely pointers to the
peculiar nature of the novel's imaginative richness, which does
not finally depend on the clues. Despite its incidental annoy-
ances and even its occasional *longueurs*, few books written in

our lifetime afford so much pleasure. Perhaps the parody-blurb at the end is not so wrong in proffering the novel as a voluminous bag of rare delights: Nabokov's garden abounds with the pleasurable visions whose artful design I have tried to sketch out here, and, as the blurb justifiably concludes, with "much, much more."

7

Nabokov for Those Who Hate Him

THE CURIOUS CASE OF *PNIN*

Pnin has often been the one Nabokov novel liked by people who dislike Nabokov, and the Nabokovians by and large have argued that the reasons such readers have been attracted to the book are the wrong ones. The litany of objections to Nabokov, sometimes rehearsed by highly intelligent readers, is a familiar one: Nabokov condescends to his readers, unless they agree to shape themselves to the mold of the ideal reader he himself has designed; his famous ingenuity, involving intricate codes and puzzles and fine-spun networks of recurring and mirroring motifs, is too ingenious by half; his stylistic and compositional virtuosity is altogether too self-admiring; the pervasive self-reflexivity of his fiction compromises the emotional engagement of the reader with the characters and their world that truly great fiction should make possible. For readers whom Nabokov usually irritates on these grounds, *Pnin* appears to be a blessed change of pace. Its protagonist is repeatedly poignant in his well-meaning, hapless ineptitude, in his loneliness, in his unrequited loves ("I have nofing left, nofing!" is his much-quoted plaintive cry);[1] and he is often not only sad but irresistibly funny—he is arguably one of the great comic characters of twentieth-century American fiction—especially in his mangling of the English language that he quixotically expects to master soon. It is no wonder that *Pnin* should have appealed to the readers of the *New Yorker*, where four of its chapters first appeared, or that it should have proved to be Nabokov's first commercial success. This is, in sum, a Nabokov novel that abundantly exhibits "human interest," a term the writer himself would have utterly deplored.

Against this perhaps soggy embrace of the novel, Nabokovians have contended that such a reading fails to see what is really going on in *Pnin*. Although it has sometimes been described as relatively unpatterned in comparison with other Nabokov novels, critical analysis (preeminently, the assiduous commentary of Gennady Barabtarlo) has abundantly shown that it is in fact elaborately patterned,[2] even if the patterns are perhaps less spectacularly displayed than in *Pale Fire* or *Ada*, and even if the touching social and emotional predicaments of the main character draw one's attention to him rather than to the patterns. It should suffice merely to recall the most salient of the complex of recurring images and motifs on which the novel is constructed: the squirrel that links Pnin's Russian childhood with the America of Waindell College in the 1950s; the French homonyms *vair* (squirrel fur) and *verre* (glass) that connect the squirrel with the reiterated invocation of glass, which in one direction leads to Victor's loving gift of the glass bowl to Pnin, in another to eyeglasses and the vocation of ophthalmology practiced by Pnin's father in St. Petersburg, and in still a third direction to mirrors, a favorite motif of Nabokov's. Then there is water, which in turn leads to mermaids and to Ophelia's death by drowning, a topic that my colleague Eric Naiman has explicated as a nexus of imaginings about sexuality and perversion.[3]

And beyond all these, there are the *de rigueur* references to butterflies.

Even the most incidental novelistic details usually prove to be implicated in these Nabokovian networks. Thus, in the train scene at the beginning, a nameless conductor makes a cameo appearance: "The conductor, a gray-headed fatherly person with steel spectacles placed rather low on his simple, functional nose and a bit of soiled adhesive tape on his thumb, had now only three coaches to deal with before reaching the last one, where Pnin rode" (p. 15). At first glance, this looks like a textbook illustration of what Roland Barthes called "the reality effect"—a piece of reality inserted into the fictional text not to mean anything but merely to signify the category of the real.[4] With the passage of time, Barthes's notion has come to seem less and less sustainable (and his own example from Flaubert's *Un coeur simple* does not really support the claim he makes about it), though perhaps the adhesive tape on the thumb might qualify. The steel spectacles sliding down the nose, on the other hand, can scarcely be dissociated from the lenses once prescribed by Pnin's father or from Pnin's own spectacles, without which he sees the world as a baffling blur. What a discerning eye can see and what a purblind eye misses is in fact a central thematic concern of the novel. The steel-rimmed spectacles of a marginal character about to vanish from the narrative, far from being merely a means to evoke a small fragment of American reality, participate in an artifice of design through which the novelist articulates meaning.

One small detail in this passing moment points not to a motif but to the social sensibility of the narrator, and that is his characterization of the conductor's "simple, functional nose." Why do we need to be told this? Though it is a rather trivial gesture, it reveals more about the narrator than about the character. It amounts to a gratuitous small act of condescension. The narrator is a man who knows what noble noses look like, aquiline noses and gently modeled noses, the nose of a Nefertiti or of a Titian Madonna, whereas this is a plebian nose, simple and functional, nothing more. Of course, at this early moment in the novel, we are insufficiently acquainted with the narrator to draw such inferences (they come with rereading), but his cumulatively insistent condescension toward the figure he likes to call "my poor Pnin" (Nabokov's working title) will eventually lead us to suspect that almost nothing he says is innocent.

It is in the character of the narrator, much discussed by critics but still warranting some sorting out, that the fluctuating status of this novel between human interest and arch self-reflexivity is especially manifested. The narrative begins with a famously deceptive lead-in. The unsuspecting reader at first may imagine that the unfolding story is told by a rather old-fashioned omniscient narrator, who by novelistic convention enjoys easy access to the thoughts and feelings of the protagonist as well as to his outward appearance and to the material details of the scene, even when no one else is present. Beginning the story in a railroad car is itself a kind of citation of the nineteenth-century novel: that is the setting in which we first meet Anna Karenina, and Virginia Woolf's memorable critique of the Edwardian novel in "Mr. Bennett and Mrs. Brown" appropriately chooses a woman traveling on a train as its exemplary instance of how realist fiction becomes entrammeled in mere surface details.

The first small hint that this is not a standard-issue omniscient narrator appears on the second page, where he measures the distance from Waindell to Cremona in versts. That, of course, marks him specifically as a Russian, and the biographical details of his Russian émigré identity will emerge in small increments as the novel proceeds. Eventually, we learn that he

met Pnin during their Russian childhood and adolescence—
though Pnin emphatically disputes his account and even claims
that everything he says is a lie, leaving us with a dizzying sense,
duly disputed by critics, of the reality of the whole world of the
novel. What appears to be indisputable from the casually reticent way in which it is reported is that the narrator had an affair
with the woman who then became Pnin's wife and that she at-
tempted suicide because of his callous treatment of her—a
chain of events to which he responded, characteristically, with
a nonchalant shrug.

The narrator is obviously meant to be a negative alter ego of
Vladimir Nabokov. He is, we learn toward the end, a successful
Anglo-Russian novelist. He has an assured mastery of English,
unlike the linguistically floundering Pnin. We don't know for
certain if he's an aristocrat, but his tone and manner sound aristocratic, in the pejorative sense. Waindell College eagerly wel-
comes him to its faculty, where he will at least in effect displace
Pnin, who fiercely rejects his offer to work under him. (Nabokov punningly remarked, as I noted earlier, that his characters
were his "galley slaves," but Pnin as character resists servitude
to the novel's narrator, himself a fictional character.) He is,
moreover, a lepidopterist, though one of his Russian acquaintances wonders whether the lepidoptery might not be an affectation. The narrator, in sum, turns out to be a thoroughly bad
actor, whatever his resemblances to the author. He is self-
congratulatory; his haughtiness toward Pnin is disagreeable; his
indifference to the consequences of his own actions is morally
reprehensible. His status as a mirror-reversal of the novelist and
definitely not the novelist himself is hinted at when among the
Russian guests at the New England country house to which
Pnin comes we encounter Sirin, Nabokov under the cover of
the pseudonym he used in the Russian phase of his career. The

ploy of introducing different splits of himself into his fiction is one that Nabokov had adopted earlier: in *The Gift,* for example, there are three different versions of the poet-novelist during his Berlin years.

The person, then, who tells Pnin's story so vividly and so engagingly is not to be trusted, and in the delicate intimation of a possibly happy ending for the chronically unhappy Pnin, the protagonist escapes the narrator, his car darting out from between the two trucks that had entrapped it and racing off to a distant horizon "where there was simply no saying what miracle might happen" (p. 191). This novel would thus seem to be an ingenious deployment of an unreliable narrator, a device Nabokov had used memorably if less subtly years earlier in *Despair.*

The characterization of the narrator I have summarized, which is more or less the standard critical account, is, it seems to me, incomplete. There are ways in which the novel's narrator, for all his moral dubiousness, speaks in Nabokov's own voice, and it is the resonance of that voice which gives depth both to the character of Pnin and to his fictional world. I am not sure whether Nabokov actually meant the narrator to be "also" Vladimir Nabokov, but I think that, despite all the narrator's suspect traits, the writer could not altogether keep him from being Vladimir Nabokov—obviously, not in his biographical profile but in his sensibility, certain of his values, his ways of perceiving the world. It may sound heretical to propose that a central feature of a book by Nabokov might not be entirely part of his conscious design, but the operation of an imaginative faculty perhaps not fully intended is what makes *Pnin* such an enchanting novel.

As a modest but characteristic instance, let us consider the narrator's take on American academic life. We know that Nabokov, constrained by material necessity to accept employment first at Wellesley and then at Cornell, worked in the academic world but was not really of it, viewing its parochialism and its benighted approaches to literature and language with satiric amusement. Here is the narrator, reporting Pnin's resistance to American ideas of how to teach foreign languages (Nabokov, one recalls, had taught Russian at Wellesley) to college students:

> . . . nor did Pnin, as a teacher, ever presume to approach the lofty gates of modern scientific linguistics, that ascetic fraternity of phonemes, that temple wherein earnest young people are taught not the language itself, but the method of teaching others to teach the language, which method, like a waterfall splashing from rock to rock, ceases to be a medium of rational investigation but perhaps in some fabulous future may become instrumental in evolving esoteric dialects—Basic Basque and so forth—spoken only by certain elaborate machines. (p. 10)

Who is speaking here? This is clearly not a direct report of Pnin's thoughts but a kind of artful extrapolation from Pnin's no doubt more inchoate attitude toward American practices of language instruction, one that gives it wit and inventive imagery that would not be available to Pnin himself. At moments like this, which abound in the novel, there is no question of the narrator's unreliability or of his bad character. To state the matter baldly—despite the critical orthodoxy that one can never state anything baldly about Nabokov—the narrator is speaking in Nabokov's own voice, expressing a view and adopting a manner that could easily be found in one of his interviews or letters. The first-person narrator (his use of "I" like the self-revelations gradually emerges) exhibits a certain narratological kinship, for all the differences, with Melville's Ishmael, who begins the book in the first person as an able-bodied seaman looking for a berth on a whaler but rapidly segues into the Shakespearian-Miltonic-biblical authorial voice that Melville needs to express the cosmic range of his prose epic. The Melvillian function of the narrator in *Pnin* is especially evident in his generalizing reflections on the human condition, his impulse to set the story of his pitiable professor in a larger frame of meaning. Thus, in the scene where Pnin experiences an alarming pain in his chest while sitting on a park bench, just before the narrator will make one of his gestures of superiority toward him ("For the nonce, I am his physician"), he offers the following thought on mortality and the frailty of the flesh:

> I do not know if it has ever been noted before that one of the main characteristics of life is discreteness. Unless a film of flesh envelops us, we die. Man exists only insofar as he is separated from his surroundings. The cranium is a space-traveler's helmet. Stay inside or you perish. Death is divestment, death is communion. It may be wonderful to mix with the landscape, but to do so is the end of the tender ego. (p. 20)

After the last sentences of this philosophic rumination, the narrator moves back to "poor Pnin" on the park bench undergoing his moment of distress. A suspicious reader might take that initial "I do not know it if has ever been noted before" as a token of the narrator's conceit, but what follows does not sustain that reading. Nabokov, with the sensibility of a gifted poet and the discipline of a taxonomic scientist, was as fond of defamiliarizing habitual patterns of thought as of defamiliarizing conventional modes of novelistic representation, and I think the reflection here on discreteness as a necessary condition of life exemplifies that fondness. "Unless a film of flesh envelops us, we die" is an arresting aphorism that exhibits no trace of the narrator's unreliability. It is put forth as a serious idea about the nature of existence, belonging to the same general category as the haunting first paragraph of *Speak, Memory* and pondered by Vladimir Nabokov, an idea for which the fictional character who is his narrator serves as conduit. The somber metaphysical wit of representing the cranium as an astronaut's helmet is of a piece with this aphorism, as is the second aphoristic declaration, strongly punctuated by alliteration: "Death is divestment, death is communion." These sentences are free of tricky mirror-games: the narrator is saying what the novelist thinks about the scary fragility and transience of human life.

The narrator in fact displays a variety of attitudes, likes and especially dislikes, that are scarcely separable from those of the author. In the paragraph immediately after the one from which I have just quoted, the narrator moves from sober reflection on mortality to satiric invention, but the presence of the novelist is equally palpable. Pnin, he reports, in the fear he may be dying, slides back mentally into his childhood, and the slippage through time occasions these observations by the narrator:

> This sensation has the sharpness of retrospective detail that is said to be the dramatic privilege of drowning individuals, especially in the former Russian Navy—a phenomenon of suffocation that a certain psychoanalyst, whose name escapes me, has explained as being the subconsciously evoked shock of one's baptism which causes an explosion of intervening recollections between the first immersion and the last. (p. 21)

The parody of psychoanalytic explanation is quite funny, and the pointed humor will be familiar to any reader of Nabokov, who conducted a lifelong campaign against what he viewed as the absurdities of psychoanalysis, in the body of his novels, in interviews, and once in a memorable brief letter to the editor of *Encounter*. The chief target of the polemic against psychoanalysis in this novel is of course the psychotherapeutic couple, Dr. Liza Wind (Pnin's ex-wife) and her husband, Dr. Eric Wind. In the group therapy sessions at the Research Bureau they create, young married women are assembled facing a team of doctors with "a secretary unobtrusively taking notes, and traumatic episodes floating out of everybody's childhood like corpses" (p. 51).

In the same paragraph, the narrator goes on to observe that "it was deadening to hear him [Dr. Wind] and Liza smacking their lips over the word 'group.'" The narrator's views in such instances are indistinguishable from Nabokov's. Indeed, the animus toward the American romance with the group touches on a fundamental principle of Nabokov's worldview: authentic thinking is the product of individual consciousness; the modern cultivation of group-think is anathema; art and literature themselves are grouped into schools or trends only by academic hacks (there is a mordant passage to this effect in *Pnin*), for the artwork, precisely like every human individual, is deeply interesting only in its distinctiveness.

Discreteness, as the narrator argues both implicitly and explicitly, clearly speaking for his author, is not only an essential condition of the self in its fragile envelope of flesh but of everything we should observe in the world we inhabit. Thus, he reports of Liza's son, who early on manifests the gift that will make him a painter, "at six, Victor already distinguished what so many adults never learn to see—the colors of shadows, the difference between the shadow of an orange and that of a plum or an avocado pear" (p. 90). The hint of elitism in "what so many adults never learn to see" is not part of the characterization of the narrator as a supercilious person because it is fully shared by Nabokov. He took great pains to deploy a finely nuanced lexicon of terms for colors (as for other things) in his fiction, and he repeatedly expressed a disdainful impatience with all those who could not see the nuances, who assembled colors into crudely conformist groups of red and green and blue.

If Nabokov's presence is readily detectable in both comic passages and in the philosophic reflections, I should add that there are moments when the two are combined, which is one of the hallmarks of his brilliance as a writer. Here, for example, is Pnin in the process of outfitting his campus office, attaching a pencil sharpener to the side of his desk: "With the help of the janitor he screwed onto the side of his desk a pencil sharpener— that highly satisfying, highly philosophic instrument that goes ticonderoga-ticonderoga, feeding on the yellow finish and sweet wood, and ends up in a kind of soundlessly ethereal void as we all must" (p. 69). Nabokov had a special interest in wooden pencils, with which he himself wrote, from the giant store-window display pencil that his mother brings him when he is bedridden with a childhood illness in *Speak, Memory* (a briefer version of that episode appears in *Pnin*) to the contemplation of pencils in *Transparent Things*. The ticonderoga sound effect of the pencil sharpener doing its work is witty and amusing, but the sharpener is also a "highly philosophic instrument" because what it does to the pencil becomes, quite suddenly, a homiletic image of the transience of life, ending in "a soundlessly ethereal void as we all must." Formally, the person speaking here is the heartless seducer and pastmaster of condescension who contributes to Pnin's expulsion from Waindell, but in effect the voice is Nabokov's, at once entertainingly defamiliarizing the world of everyday objects and seriously meditating on the ephemerality of human life.

The obvious objection to what I have been saying about the Nabokov face of the fictional narrator is that it does not address what is essential to this novel. It is hardly surprising that a narrator who shares some prominent biographical features with the author, and who is, inescapably, the author's vehicle for representing and reflecting on the world, should express attitudes scarcely distinguishable from those of the author about psychoanalysis, American academic types, the public lecture circuit, and even mortality and life's brevity. The center of the novel, however, is a character named Pnin, and careful readers have repeatedly noticed that the narrator's treatment of him is morally shabby, conducted from the viewpoint of unwarranted superiority of a fictional character invented by Vladimir Nabokov. All this is self-evidently true, but it is a truth with a writ that does not extend as far in the world of the novel as has sometimes been thought. Let me cite one substantial passage from the end of the first chapter that provides a kind of frame for how we see Pnin in what follows. Pnin, finally arrived at his lecture in Cremona, is waiting to speak while his introducer, Judith Clyde, "an ageless blonde in aqua rayon," inanely drones on. His attention lapses and his consciousness slips back into another world.

In the middle of the front row of seats he saw one of his Baltic aunts, wearing the pearls and the lace and the blond wig she had worn at all the performances of the great ham actor Khodotov, whom she had adored from afar before drifting into insanity. Next to her, shyly smiling, sleek dark head inclined, gentle brown gaze shining up at Pnin from under velvet eyebrows, sat a dead sweetheart of his, fanning herself with a program. Murdered, forgotten, unrevenged, immortal, many old friends were scattered through the dim hall among more recent people, such as Miss Clyde, who had modestly regained a front seat. Vanya Bednyashkin, shot by the Reds in 1919 because his father was a Liberal, was gaily signaling to his former schoolmate from the back of the hall. And in an inconspicuous situation Dr. Pavel Pnin and his anxious wife, both a little blurred but on the whole wonderfully recovered from their obscure dissolution, looked at their son with the same life-consuming passion and pride that they had looked at him with that night in 1912 when, at a school festival, commemorating Napoleon's defeat, he had recited (a bespectacled lad all alone on the stage) a poem by Pushkin. (pp. 27–28)

This ghostly apparition of vanished souls dissolves, with Miss Clyde now seen receiving compliments on her speech from someone next to her, "while from behind that body another twinkling old party was thrusting into her field of vision a pair of withered, soundlessly clapping hands." On this spectral note the first chapter concludes.

In this passage, at any rate, the narrator exhibits not condescension but profound empathy with Pnin. Let me try to tease out what is involved in that empathy, because it may help us understand why Pnin is such a touching figure. The cast of Russian friends and relations who float up in the rows of the Cremona lecture hall shows one antic touch that might accord with the narrator's satiric view of Pnin—the blond-wigged aunt, destined to lose her mind, who is a groupie of the oxymoronically noted "great ham actor Khodotov." But, then, every family has its oddballs and wayward types, so the odd aunt contributes to the verisimilar representation of the remembered family. A good deal of Nabokov's writing from early to late is about loss, for a whole set of rather obvious biographical reasons, from the initial exile to his father's murder. He firmly resisted being maudlin about his losses, but he was certainly haunted by them. In *Speak, Memory*, he found a way both to register loss and to overcome it brilliantly in the act of writing. *Speak, Memory* abounds in moments when the present metamorphoses into the past, though they work differently than this appearance of ghosts in the lecture hall. They are far more volitional, the writer's evocative art producing the fullness of the past recaptured through finely directed memory rather than through some sort of Proustian involuntary memory. In the present instance, the narrator, himself an exile and the spokesman for his exiled author, evinces compassionate understanding for Pnin, an awkward guest in an alien cultural setting, as the character sees the faces of those from whom he has been irrevocably severed. Much of what makes Pnin so affecting is his brave determination to carry on in the persistent aching awareness of all his losses, making a happy little party for his Waindell acquaintances, clinging to the dream of producing a work of scholarship, loving the son of his ex-wife, probably even still loving her despite her unflagging rejection of him. The narrator, even with his proclivity to condescension, empathically knows this about Pnin (knows it as Vladimir Nabokov) and invites us to participate in that knowledge.

The mention of the dead sweetheart here is especially revelatory in this regard. She is presumably Mira—despite the formulation, "a dead sweetheart of his," which might imply one of several—about whom we hear more later in the novel. The way she is evoked, "shyly smiling, sleek dark head inclined, gentle brown gaze shining up at Pnin under velvet eyebrows," shows no trace of irony. The very next sentence begins with the word "murdered," which refers to the victims of Bolshevik terror but also reflects back on the dead sweetheart, who, if she is Mira, perished in a Nazi concentration camp. Pnin at this juncture is by no means the figure of fun that the narrator is wont to present him as being; instead, we are invited to enter momentarily into his sad, still-loving memory of the woman lost to him and then destroyed through totalitarian violence. Though she appears in the novel only in a couple of brief fragments, she is, after all, the radiant counterfactual alternative to the dully psychoanalytic and unfeeling Liza Wind, the woman Pnin actually married.

There is genuine sentiment here but not, I think, sentimentality. The nicety of feeling is in part enabled by the fact that Nabokov does not linger over the loving memory but conveys it through a few fleeting images, and he is also careful to have his narrator maintain a witty awareness that this is all an evanescent hallucination, as when he describes the parents appearing "both a little blurred but on the whole wonderfully recovered from their obscure dissolution." The concluding image of the child Pnin reciting Pushkin at a patriotic event perfectly rounds out this sympathetic picture. Bespectacled then as now, in the presence of his proud parents, he stands on a stage, as in the narrative present he stands on another stage, without parents, without family, virtually without friends, addressing an audience that is no doubt amused and probably also baffled by his preposterous English.

In most practical matters, Pnin is conspicuous for his ineptitude, and as such he is both a butt of humor and an object of compassion (at least for the reader). In matters of feeling and moral sensibility, he is consistently apt, much the superior not only of the narrator but of almost everyone around him in Waindell. When he recites to his sympathetic colleague Hagen a small catalog of atrocities from Nicholas the First to the Armenian genocide and colonialism in Africa and concludes, "The history of man is the history of pain!" (p. 168), he expresses a morally resonant perception that no one else in the novel is capable of making. What concerns Pnin about history equally concerns the Nabokov of *Invitation to a Beheading, Bend Sinister, Pale Fire,* and a good many other texts. In just this connection, a conversation with a certain Madame Shpolyanksi forces Pnin to remember Mira Belochkin, despite the regimen of self-protective forgetting he had clung to ever since he learned of her death:

> One had to forget—because one could not live with the thought that this graceful, fragile, tender young woman with those eyes, that smile, those gardens and snows in the background, had been brought in a cattle car to an extermination camp and killed by an injection of phenol into the heart, into the gentle heart one had heard beating under one's lips in the dark of the past. And since the exact form of Mira's death had not been recorded, Mira kept dying a great number of deaths in one's mind, and undergoing a great number of resurrections, only to die again and again, led away by a trained nurse, inoculated with filth, tetanus bacilli, broken glass, gassed in a sham shower bath with prussic acid, burned alive in a pit on a gasoline-soaked pile of beechwood. (p. 135)

This wrenching passage has been recalled by many readers of the novel, but in regard to the narrator's relationship with Pnin that we have been considering, it is worth observing what role the narrator plays in it. There is, of course, no irony, no condescension, no gestures toward "my poor friend Pnin." Quite the contrary. Let us note the insistent use of "one" in the passage, especially in "the gentle heart one had heard beating under one's lips in the dark of the past." The reiterated "one" is even a little awkward, at least to an American ear though perhaps less so to a British ear because of the greater prevalence of the usage in polite English circles. I would suppose that behind this "one" lies the French *on*, which in that language is a perfectly natural substitution in the active voice for a passive form. In any case, there is a strategic point in Nabokov's deployment of "one" here. The obvious alternative would have been to use the third-person singular, but to say "he" would have had the effect of clearly defining the experience as uniquely belonging to Pnin. If this passage is free indirect discourse—I'm not at all sure that it is—perhaps Pnin is trying to distance the memory by adopting an impersonal form. The more likely explanation is that the use of "one" allows a merging of Pnin and the narrator. It was of course Pnin who heard Mira's gentle heart beating as he kissed her breast (an act clearly implied), but the narrator is in a sense there with him, imagining in the heat of empathic identification the rapture of kissing so sweet a woman and the anguish of being constantly pursued by the horrific alternate images of her death. The narrator at this juncture is certainly not the unfeeling seducer of Pnin's future wife or the successful émigré novelist with pretensions to superiority. He is the voice of the author, a man wracked by the consciousness of all that an age of mass-murdering totalitarianism has perpetrated on innocent people, including people he loved or perhaps could have loved. Pnin in the persistent pangs he feels over Mira Belochkin's fate is a moral everyman—even a moral hero—of his dark times, and those who read him that way are not, I think, guilty of sentimentality.

The character Pnin is a rare fusion of disparate elements—sad, doomed to failure, an awkward denizen of an alien world, an inadvertent source of hilarity, and morally noble. The enabling device for this richly multiple characterization is precisely Nabokov's inconsistency in his treatment of the narrator.

It is hard to know to what extent the inconsistency may have been by design, but it seems clear that the novelist could not resist giving the narrator an intermittent presence not as the complacent *littérateur* but as Nabokov, and without that he could hardly have done what he wanted with Pnin and his difficult fate. It may well be, as Galya Diment has suggested to me, that the serial publication of a substantial part of this novel contributed to these inconsistencies in the handling of the narrator—inconsistencies that, as I have been arguing, actually enrich the book. Nabokov's own self-image as a writer, of course, was the exquisite Flaubertian artificer, exercising perfect control over all his materials through painstaking revision. In this one instance, he makes happy contact instead with a Dickensian model, in which the novelist improvises from episode to episode, conscious of his continuing audience.

I would like to offer a final example that is not as emotionally fraught as Pnin's recollection of the murdered Mira. Pnin has just spent a long afternoon in the college library:

> Doffing his spectacles, he rubbed with the knuckles of the hand that had held them his naked and tired eyes and, still in thought, fixed his mild gaze on the window above, where, gradually, through his dissolving meditation, there appeared the violet-blue air of dark, silver-tooled by the reflection of the fluorescent lights of the ceiling, and, among spidery black twigs, a mirrored row of bright book spines. (p. 78)

This is not a passage steeped in significance, and it certainly has no importance in the unfolding of the plot. We have encountered before these spectacles of Pnin's, myopic son of an ophthalmologist. These few sentences effectively represent his myopia, like a cinematographer's use of a Vaseline-smeared lens to produce a similar effect. We are reminded of how helpless

Pnin is without his glasses, though even with them he fails to see much of what he should that is going on around him. The visual interaction of the blue twilight air and the fluorescent ceiling lights makes the blue "silver-tooled," giving birth for the moment to an exquisite artifact fashioned from light. The maneuver of reflection is quintessentially Nabokovian, its intertwining of exterior and interior a small anticipation of the famous image with which the poem "Pale Fire" begins. The rows of books on the shelves are reflected in the library window where they mingle with the black twigs outside, and the effect of mingling is no doubt enhanced by the blurring medium of Pnin's shortsightedness through which everything is seen. One might argue that this scene is introduced in the novel because Nabokov loved to conjure such optical displays. But perhaps we should allow for the possibility that the writer, in the guise of his sometimes sympathetic and always aesthetically accomplished narrator, has accorded his protagonist a moment of grace. Pnin, after a bout of hard labor in the mines of scholarship, removes for the nonce the spectacles that are his necessary instrument and is vouchsafed a moment of unanticipated beauty, blue etched with silver, inside and outside in mysterious consort. We are made repeatedly aware that Pnin is a person struggling, often quite comically, with an onerous destiny—rejected, lonely, sometimes mocked. But his perfect moral authenticity as a man of feeling makes him deserving of some moments of grace, and in the curious narrative workings of this novel, it is the narrator, his chief mocker, who from time to time gives him his due, helping us perceive his essential human dignity.

Viktor Shklovsky once provocatively described *Tristram Shandy* as "the most typical novel of world literature."[5] In an analogous vein, one might characterize the ostensibly anomalous

Pnin as the most typical novel of Nabokov's oeuvre. The relation of the ambiguous narrator to the hapless protagonist may in fact illuminate the role of the narrator (or, in any case, the implied author) elsewhere in Nabokov's fiction. On reflection, the implicit moral perspective in *Lolita,* in *Ada,* and in many other of his novels is not that of a heartless literary artificer but of someone whose imaginative sympathy is with the vulnerable and the victimized—not with Humbert Humbert but with the abused Lolita, not with Van Veen but with the drowned Lucette. *Pnin* is obviously one of Nabokov's most touching and most amusing novels, but it may also be one of the most instructive about the nature of his moral imagination.

8

Invitation to a Beheading

NABOKOV AND THE ART
OF POLITICS

The logical result of Fascism is the introduction of aesthetics
into politics. . . . Mankind's self-alienation has reached such a
degree that it can experience its own destruction as an
aesthetic pleasure of the first order.

—WALTER BENJAMIN, "THE WORK OF ART IN THE
AGE OF MECHANICAL REPRODUCTION"

Because *Invitation to a Beheading* is in many ways the most explicit of Nabokov's fictions of ostentatious artifice, it at once
lucidly illustrates his conception of the novel and puts to the
test the limits of that conception. With the publication by stages
in English of all of Nabokov's Russian fiction, and with a growing body of intelligent American criticism on his novels, the
brilliance of his technical virtuosity has come to be widely ap-
preciated, but a suspicion persists in some critical circles that
his achievement is mere technical virtuosity, that the intricately
convoluted designs of his novels make them self-enclosed, sterile, and therefore finally "minor." What is at issue is not just a

critical commitment to realism—a literary convention toward which Nabokov has shown both lofty disdain and impish mockery—but an expectation of moral seriousness in literature that goes back in English criticism to figures like Matthew Arnold and Samuel Johnson. For American and British critics deriving from this tradition, the novel, though it may and perhaps even should delight, must above all teach us something—about the social, political, and spiritual spheres we inhabit, about the nature of moral choice and character, about the complexities of our psychological makeup. The obviously centripetal direction, then, of Nabokov's imagination, whirling all social, political, and psychological materials into a circumscribed inner concern with art and the artist, is construed as a failure of the novelist to engage the larger world of human experience, and would seem to confess his ultimate lack of seriousness. *Invitation to a Beheading* is surely an extreme instance of this general centripetal movement. Written in Berlin in 1935, it takes the ugliest, most disturbing of modern political actualities, the totalitarian state, and uses it, one gathers, merely as a dramatically convenient background for the recurrent Nabokovian theme, which is, to borrow Simon Karlinsky's apt formulation, "the nature of the creative imagination and the solitary, freak-like role into which a man gifted with such imagination is inevitably cast in any society."[1]

The narrator of *Invitation to a Beheading* plays so continually and conspicuously with the status of his narration as artifice that the general point hardly needs critical elaboration. The first paragraph of the novel informs us that the protagonist has been sentenced to die, and immediately the narrator pauses to remind us that we are reading a book, and a rather peculiar one at that: "So we are nearing the end. The right-hand, still untasted part of the novel . . . has suddenly, for no reason at all, become quite meager: a few minutes of quick reading, already downhill, and—O horrible!"[2] In the conventional novel of imprisonment, in the conventional fictional pattern of crime and punishment, the sentencing of the hero would of course take place toward the end, after a long and arduous development, so we are put on notice at once that conventional expectations will be subverted in the particular fiction before us. As we move on, Nabokov takes pains to remind us repeatedly that each scene has been arranged by a theatrical stage manager: again and again, visual descriptions are conveyed in explicitly painterly terms, even made to seem two-dimensional painted backdrops; if there is an atmospheric disturbance, it has to be reported as "a summer thunderstorm, simply yet tastefully staged, . . . performed outside" (p. 129); and time itself, as Cincinnatus points out, is not a continuous flow, like time in the "real" world, but purely a series of conventional indications within a represented action: "note the clock in the corridor. The dial is blank; however, every hour the watchman washes off the old hand and daubs on a new one—and that's how we live, by tarbrush time" (p. 135). And so the novel proceeds, through dozens of ingenious variations on this one underlying idea, down to the grand finale when the daubed-in perspective slips out of kilter, the scenery totters, the painted rows of spectators come crashing down, and Cincinnatus goes striding off toward what we hope is a more human world.

All this flaunted artifice is clear enough in the novel, and it makes good thematic sense in relation to the hero, whose unspeakable sin of "gnostic turpitude" consists, after all, in imagining the world as an artist and in wanting to become what the world he exists in cannot by its nature tolerate, a true writer. It is precisely this continual concern, however, with the artist's predicament that the devotees of high seriousness object to in

Nabokov. Hasn't the writer shirked his responsibilities by converting totalitarianism into the stuff of a fable about art and artifice? Can there be anything but frivolous self-indulgence in his decision finally to collapse the totalitarian state into mere discarded stage machinery, at the very moment in history when all civilized values were threatened by Stalinist terror and Nazi murderous hatred?

Such objections, it seems to me, conceive in far too narrow terms the ways in which fiction may "engage the world of experience," or are predicated on rather restrictive notions of what is involved in experience—even political experience. I would argue on the contrary that there is an important inner connection between the special emphasis on ostentatious artifice in *Invitation to a Beheading* and the totalitarian world that is the setting of the novel, and that Nabokov, precisely through his concern for art and the fate of the artist, is able to illuminate a central aspect of the supposedly human condition in an era of police states and totalitarian terrors. Two years after writing *Invitation to a Beheading*, Nabokov included in *The Gift* a kind of meditation about the meaning of executions that could serve as a useful gloss on the entire nature of political and social reality in the earlier novel:

Fyodor recalled his father saying that innate in every man is the feeling of something insuperably abnormal about the death penalty, something like the uncanny reversal of action in a looking-glass that makes everyone left-handed: not for nothing is everything reversed for the executioner: the horse-collar is put on upside down when the robber Razin is taken to the scaffold; wine is poured for the headsman not with a natural turn of the wrist but backhandedly; and if, according to the Swabian code, an insulted actor was permitted to seek satisfaction by striking the shadow of the offender, in China it was precisely an actor—a shadow who fulfilled the duties of the executioner, and responsibility being as it were lifted from the world of men and transformed into the inside-out one of mirrors.[3]

Now, in order to make sense of this seemingly fanciful notion, we shall have to raise the tactless question of what, in fact, Nabokov conceives reality to be. This would appear to be particularly foolish to ask of a writer who has warned that reality is a dubious label for what the mind constructs around it, but I believe it is of the utmost relevance to Nabokov's whole literary enterprise, the ultimate concerns of which are epistemological and metaphysical—like those of his great English precursor in the fiction of ostentatious artifice, Laurence Sterne. Nabokov, like Sterne, is continually bemused by the mystery through which individual consciousness in a subtle and at times perverse alchemic process transmutes the brute data of experience into the "reality" that each of us inhabits.

The key to any sense of reality, certainly for Nabokov and probably for all of us, is the perception of pattern. Consciousness needs at least the illusion that it can control some of the data it encounters, seeing in them orderly sequence, recurrence, analogy, cause and effect, in order to be able to believe in their reality: the sun sets, the sun also rises, says the Preacher in Ecclesiastes, but if it never rose again, if it came up as a thousand incandescent fireballs or a great gleaming poppy-seed cake, we would be in a nightmare or a fun-house fantasy, not in what most of us would call the real world. For Nabokov, as consciousness achieves a condition of acrobatic poise and elastic strength, integrating more and more into meaningful patterns, it encounters more reality, or rather makes the world around it at last real.

That is why Cincinnatus, trapped in a world that he repeatedly reminds us is a bad jumble of "senseless visions, bad dreams, dregs of delirium, the drivel of nightmares" (p. 36), is not an escapist but a defiant rebel when he envisages another existence comprising perfect, endlessly delighting pattern: "'There, tam, là-bas, the gaze of men glows with inimitable understanding; there the freaks that are tortured here walk unmolested; there time takes shape according to one's pleasure, like a figured rug whose folds can be gathered in such a way that two designs will meet" (p. 94). The most prominent literary echo here is of course Baudelaire's vision of perfected art and pleasure in *"L'Invitation au voyage"*—"Là tout n'est qu'ordre et beauté, / Luxe, calme et volupté" (There, all is pure order and beauty, / Sumptuousness, calm, and pleasure)—while those artfully gathered folds of patterned time nicely characterize Nabokov's subsequent treatment of time in *Speak, Memory*, his attempt to fix through art the reality of his personal experience, and in fact he invokes the same image of the patterned rug there. What may seem peculiar is the obtrusion into Cincinnatus's vision of aesthetic bliss of an explicitly moral idea, that in the harmonious world elsewhere the poor tormented freaks of his own flawed world will be left unharmed. To begin to understand this interweaving of the moral and the aesthetic, we must return to the shadowy headsman of Fyodor's father's reflections, who stands still unexplained in his backhanded, inside-out realm of mirrors.

If consciousness is the medium through which reality comes into being, the sudden and final obliteration of consciousness through mechanical means is the supreme affirmation by human agents—the executioners—of the principle of unreality. For the mind's ability to perceive freely or create patterns and delight in them is what makes a person's life human, but in the appointed executioner, mind is focused down to guiding the motions that will blot out all pattern in another human mind, man in a grim farce pretending that he is not a sentient being but something like a falling tree or an avalanche, a stupid instrument of blind, murderous forces. Execution is the central rite of Cincinnatus's world, realizing its utmost possibilities, because that world, in all its institutional arrangements and daily social relations, is explicitly contrived to numb, cloud, cripple, and finally extirpate individual consciousness. It therefore must remain a relentlessly incredible world from the viewpoint of any genuinely human consciousness—its halls filled with trick mirrors producing meretricious effects, its personages crudely painted clowns more papier-mâché than flesh, even the conventional spider in its prison cell turning out to be a rubber facsimile, the shoddy practical joke of a dime-store mentality. Here, as elsewhere, Nabokov's antirealist method has the effect of probing to the roots of real experience: his totalitarian state is not in any sense a disguised description of an actual regime, but the lineaments of his fictional fantasy, drawn with a rigorous sense of self-consistency (and not freely improvised like the fictions of some American "fantasts"), reveal the ultimate implications of the totalitarian principle, constitute a kind of ideal model of totalitarian possibilities. Thus, Julian Moynihan could with considerable justice see in this novel a prophetic insight into the underlying operative assumption in Hitler's enterprise of mass-manufactured death: "The unspoken, vile, dehumanizing assumption that the guiltless victim must collaborate in his own torture and death, must enter into the corruption of his tormentors and depart this world robbed of life, integrity and individuality alike."[4] What must be added is that this world of ultimate obscenity is deliberately, justifiably held at a comic distance so that the horror does not overwhelm, so that the whole insidious mechanism can be examined by a humane critical intelligence that affirms its own power to prevail through its constant presence in the cunning concern of the narrator for the embattled humanity of his protagonist. If the observer is able to preserve an intelligent sense of the possibilities of consciousness, then a society based on a universal collusion to surrender consciousness must seem to him a grotesque and improbable farce, a congeries of "specters, werewolves, parodies" that is sinister in both senses of the word— menacing and belonging to a left-handed, inverted realm of mere negation.

It is worth examining more closely the relation between the theme of art in the foreground and the political background of the novel. Sartre's dictum that "a novelist's aesthetic always sends us back to his metaphysic" is eminently applicable here, and I think it is also relevant to keep in mind Sartre's rather special sense of "metaphysic," which implies not merely a conceptual grasp of reality but a moral posture toward it. Even what seems to be a preoccupation with the mechanics of technique on Nabokov's part has a strict thematic function, and this is especially true of a recurrent peculiarity of *Invitation to a Beheading*—that so many of its scenes are conceived as formal exercises in vision. Here, for example, is a brief description of the prisoner futilely attempting to see out of his cell window:

> Cincinnatus was standing on tiptoe, holding the iron bars with his small hands, which were all white from the strain, and half of his face was covered with a sunny grating, and the

gold of his left mustache shone, and there was a tiny golden cage in each of his mirrorlike pupils, while below, from behind, his heels rose out of the too-large slipper. (p. 29)

The physical image of Cincinnatus is of course sharply and meticulously defined, made to seem very "real"—and not only the physical image, because through that final, telling detail of the oversize slippers we get a sense of the sad, touching, pathetic, vaguely funny nature of this trapped figure. What is important to note is that virtually every phrase of the description makes us aware of the cunning artificer: framing, selecting, eliciting patterns. Nabokov in effect invites us to participate in the perception of how a painter (a Flemish realist, let us say) and, by implication, a novelist, goes about "realizing" a scene. Each of the minute details, the small hands white with gripping, the gleaming half-mustache, the bars reflected in the pupils, is strategically chosen to make us see the whole figure caught in a particular light and a particular posture. We are led simultaneously to envisage Cincinnatus as a human being in a moment of anguish and as a formal study in dark and light contrasts, symmetrically divided by shadow. The reflecting surface is of course an invaluable resource in such studies of the possibilities of representation—one recalls the mirrors in Van Eyck interiors, much admired by Nabokov—because it allows the artist to duplicate forms and objects on a different scale, from a different angle, or even to smuggle new presences into the scene. The golden cages, however, in Cincinnatus's eyes are more than a device of visual preciosity, for in our very awareness of their paradoxical beauty we are led back to the terror of Cincinnatus's entrapment: is the cage in fact inside his head, a function of his own mode of vision, or, alternately, has an actual imprisonment cut him off from reality, reducing vision to an infinite regress of unyielding bars, so that, in the lines from Rilke about a caged panther that we have seen to be relevant to Humbert Humbert, "Ihm ist, als ob es tausend Stäben gäbe, / Und hinter tausend Stäben keine Welt" (For him, it's as though there were a thousand bars, / and behind a thousand bars no world)?

Let us look at another, more elaborate instance of these exercises in vision. Cincinnatus frequently thinks back to the shreds of happiness he was able to grasp in the Tamara Gardens; it is the one place in which he can imagine concretely something like a human environment. But it should be noted that even in nostalgia he does not simply recall the gardens, he explicitly *envisages* them. At one point he is brought out by his captors onto the turret of the prison and looks down on the town below:

> Our travelers found themselves on a broad terrace at the top of a tower, whence there was a breathtaking view, since not only was the tower huge, but the whole fortress towered hugely on the crest of a huge cliff, of which it seemed to be a monstrous outgrowth. Far below one could see the almost vertical vineyards, and the creamy road that wound down to the dry river bed; a tiny person in red was crossing the convex bridge; the speck running in front of him was most likely a dog. Further away the sun-flooded town described an ample hemicycle: some of the varicolored houses proceeded in even rows, accompanied by round trees, while others, awry, crept down slopes, stepping on their own shadows; one could distinguish the traffic moving on First Boulevard, and an amethystine shimmer at the end, where the famous fountain played; and still further, toward the hazy folds of the hills that formed the horizon, there was the dark stipple of oak groves, with, here and there, a pond gleaming like a hand

mirror, while other bright ovals of water gathered, glowing through the tender mist, over there to the west, where the serpentine Strop had its source. Cincinnatus, his palm pressed to his cheek, in motionless, ineffably vague and perhaps even blissful despair, gazed at the glimmer and haze of the Tamara Gardens and at the dove-blue melting hills beyond them—oh, it was a long time before he could take his eyes away. (pp. 42–43)

If the passage demonstrates a rigorous adherence to consistent point of view, it is point of view more in the sense of a Breughel than a Henry James. The paradoxical effectiveness of the description, like that of Cincinnatus clinging to the bars, depends on our awareness that the scene seems real precisely because it is a scrupulously ordered artistic composition. As we look down on the scene with Cincinnatus, we are taken into the magic of its presence by being made to see it as a painting. The foreground is defined, in a painterly repetition of form, as a duplication in outline with diminished scale—a huge tower on a fortress towering hugely on a cliff. The eye is then led down through the most careful arrangement of perspective along the winding road (formally duplicated further down in the serpentine line of the river), past the tiny human figure on the convex bridge and the indistinguishable speck, which is "most likely a dog," on to the town itself and the bluish haze of the hills at the horizon. Effects of color and light are nicely balanced in painterly fashion and conveyed to us in a vocabulary that suggests the artist's nuanced choice of pigments and even something of the way he applies them to his canvas: we move from the "creamy" road to the red figure, then into the "sun-flooded" town with its "varicolored" houses, set off by the "hazy folds of the hills" in the distance and the "dark stipple" of the woods just below the hills. The vocabulary of color is not only precise in its distinctions but also designed to communicate a sense of the pleasure—an almost sensual delight in the opulence of beauty—that informs aesthetic experience: this is why the road is "creamy," the distant fountain an "amethystine shimmer" in the sunlight, the horizon an inviting vision of "dove-blue melting hills." Inevitably, there are reflecting surfaces in the picture, those ponds seen gleaming like hand mirrors in the park far below, the mirror here serving the rather simple function of illustrating the artist's exquisite ordering of effects of light and perspective in the scene. Finally, there is one detail in the landscape that goes beyond the decorum of painterly terms, the houses creeping down the slope, "stepping on their own shadows." This graphic personification, however, seems perfectly right because it suggests how a scene done with painstaking art begins to transcend the limits of its own medium, assuming an elusive life that is more than color and line, plane and texture.

Such passages offer ample evidence of Nabokov's virtuosity, but looking at them, as we have so far, out of context, we have not yet answered the question of what it is all for. These scenes actually stand in a relation of dialectic tension to the world of the novel in which they occur, and one clear indication of that is the artful placement of mirrors within them. Fyodor's father in *The Gift*, we recall, uses mirrors in a negative sense, connecting them with death and unreality, but in *Invitation to a Beheading* there are good and bad uses of mirrors, just as there is good and bad art. Nabokov invokes a whole spectrum of traditional symbolic associations suggested by mirrors—the mirror of art held to nature; the mirror of consciousness "reflecting" reality (or does it only reflect itself, we are at least led to wonder—is Cincinnatus's prison merely a house of mirrors?); the mirror as a depthless, inverted, unreal, mocking imitation of the real world. The most striking development of the mirror idea in the novel is appropriately ambiguous, Nabokov's memorable parable of imagination and reality, the crazily rippled "nonnon mirrors," which, when set opposite complementarily shapeless lumps, reflect beautifully "real" forms, the two negatives making a positive. Is this a model for the alchemy that the imagination works on formless reality, or does it rather illustrate the kind of mountebank's trick that has come to serve as a manufactured substitute for art, a merely illusionistic amusement for the masses? The former alternative, in which one can see the distorted magical mirrors as an image of Nabokov's own art, is clearly the more attractive of the two, but the fact that the device of the nonnons is reported to us by Cincinnatus's mother, herself the tricky insubstantial creature of a dimensionless world, at any rate leaves a teasing residue of doubt in our minds.

Elsewhere in the novel, the contexts in which mirrors appear are more clearly negative. For the insidious M'sieur Pierre, they are the implements of a self-admiring, self-absorbed hedonism: "There is nothing more pleasant," he tells Cincinnatus, laying claim to a background of worldly sexual expertise, "than to surround oneself with mirrors and watch the good work going on there" (p. 145). For Marthe, Cincinnatus's inexhaustibly promiscuous wife, the mirror is the most patently fake stage prop in her factitious world of theatrical (or rather farcical) deceptions: as part of the domestic scenery that she has temporarily moved into Cincinnatus's cell, "There came a mirrored wardrobe, bringing with it its own private reflection (namely, a corner of the connubial bedroom with a stripe of sunlight across the floor, a dropped glove, and an open door in the distance)" (p. 99).

More ambiguously, Cincinnatus himself adopts the tricky role of the mirror as a stratagem of survival: a mirror is of course a transparent surface with an opaque backing, and Cincinnatus, an opaque figure in a world of mutually transparent souls, learns to "feign translucence, employing a complex system of optical illusions, as it were" (p. 24), that is, reflecting to those around him a fleeting simulacrum of translucence from the surface of his immutable opacity.

It is precisely the association of mirrors with both art and consciousness that justifies this range of ambiguities in their appearance in the novel. For while Cincinnatus dreams of, and at certain moments his creator pointedly exercises, a beautifully patterned art, the most essential quality of the world that imprisons him is cheap, false, meretricious, mechanical art. More succinctly, Nabokov's ideal model of the totalitarian state is, to invoke the embracing Russian term he explains so elaborately in his study of Gogol, a world of *poshlust,* which, in drastic shorthand, might be thought of as the fake sublime.[5] The leering, inane faces of *poshlust* are everywhere in *Invitation to a Beheading,* but I will try briefly to review some of the most symptomatic instances. The act of murder by state decree is imagined by its perpetrators as a work of art. M'sieur Pierre fancies himself an *artiste,* carrying his headsman's ax in a velvet-lined case like a musical instrument. In his person and manner M'sieur Pierre is obviously the embodiment of quintessential *poshlust,* often with excruciating detail, as in the two illusionistic green leaves he has tattooed around his left nipple to make it seem "a rosebud ... of marchpane and candied angelica" (p. 160). The eve of Cincinnatus's execution is marked by a grandiose ceremony that smacks of a crucifixion staged in Radio City Music Hall with a thousand dancing Rockettes. A million varicolored light bulbs are planted "artfully" (the narrator's word) in the grass to form a monogram of the initials of the headsman and his victim. The chief ingredients of this "art" are monstrous quantity and mechanical means; appropriately, the production is sloppily arranged and doesn't quite come off.

Bad art, in fact, is the ubiquitous instrument of torture for the imprisoned Cincinnatus. Thus, in a niche in the prison corridor, he sees what he imagines is a window through which he will be able to look down on the longed-for Tamara Gardens in the town below, but when he approaches, he discovers that it is a crude trompe l'oeil painting: "This landscape, daubed in several layers of distance, executed in blurry green hues and illuminated by concealed bulbs, was reminiscent . . . of the backdrop in front of which a wind orchestra toils and puffs" (p. 76). The colors are drab, the treetops stirless, the lighting torpid; in short, the painting is in every respect the exact opposite of that artfully composed view of the town and the gardens that Cincinnatus had enjoyed earlier from the prison tower.

The use of hidden light bulbs as part of an unconvincingly illusionistic effect is significant because the substitution of mechanical device for imagination is the key to most of the bad art in the novel. Thus, the art par excellence of this world of *poshlust* is photography. It is essential to the grand production on the eve of the beheading that Cincinnatus and his executioner be photographed together by flashbulb light (predictably, with hideous results). At the beginning of the novel, two local newspapers with two weirdly complementary color photographs of the prisoner's house on the front page are brought to him (and one should keep in mind, of course, the inevitably false, blurry, bleeding quality of color photographs reproduced on newsprint in the era when this novel was written). One picture shows the façade of the house, with the photographer from the second paper peering out of Marthe's bedroom window. The other, taken from that window, shows the garden and gate with the first photographer shooting the façade of the house. The circularity of the two photographs is just the reverse of Nabokov's practice of introducing hints of his own presence as artificer into his fictions. Here each of the photographers is inadvertently caught by the other in the act of using his mechanical black box to snap the scene, and the tawdry nature of the whole procedure is emphasized by the clear hint of still another sexual betrayal by Marthe in the presence of the photographer in her bedroom.

The culminating example of the mechanical art of photography as the instrument of *poshlust* is the "photohoroscope" devised by M'sieur Pierre. Using retouched snapshots of Emmie, the young daughter of the warden, placing her face in montage with photographs of older people in other circumstances, he offers a chronological record of a hypothetical woman's life, from childhood to old age and death (pp. 167–171). The simulation of a life is of course utterly unconvincing, and there is something vaguely obscene about this face of a little girl faked up as the face of a mature woman, then of an old lady. The photohoroscope is an ultimate achievement of anti-art, using purely mechanical means to produce a patently false contrivance, impotent to cope with the rich enigma of experience in time, blind to the dimension of consciousness, profaning the mystery of human life. The companion piece to M'sieur Pierre's album is the novel *Quercus* that Cincinnatus takes out of the prison library. This three-thousand-page tome on the life of an oak tree, "considered to be the acme of modern thought," is Nabokov's reductio ad absurdum of the naturalistic novel and of the principle of exhaustive documentary realism:

It seemed as though the author were sitting with his camera somewhere among the topmost branches of the Quercus, spying out and catching his prey. Various images of life would come and go, pausing among the green macules of light. The normal periods of inaction were filled with scientific descriptions of the oak itself, from the viewpoints of dendrology, ornithology, coleopterology, mythology—or popular descriptions, with touches of folk humor. (p. 123)

Such photographic realism, in other words, is mindless, formless, pointless, infinitely tedious, devoid of humanity. It denies imagination, spontaneity, the shaping power of human consciousness; subverting everything art should be, it produces the perfect novel of a totalitarian world.

At this point seekers of high seriousness might be moved to object: a merely aesthetic critique of totalitarianism, an objection to it on the grounds of its bad taste? This novel does offer an aesthetic critique of the totalitarian idea, but it is not "merely" that because so much more than good taste is implied by art for Nabokov. As I shall now try to make clear, Nabokov's aesthetic in fact leads us back to a metaphysic, and one with ultimately moral implications. In his discussion of *poshlust* apropos of Gogol's *Dead Souls*, Nabokov remarks parenthetically that it is a quality "which yawns universally at times of revolution or war" (p. 65). I am tempted to see a Popean pun in "yawns," like the great apocalyptic pun near the end of the *Dunciad* in which Dulness yawns—both announcing the soporific reign of universal tedium and threatening to engulf civilization. In any case, the world of Pope's *Dunciad* offers a suggestive analogy to that of *Invitation to a Beheading*, being a hilarious yet ominous farce that represents a general breakdown of humanistic values, where the intellect is put to such widespread perverted use that art and thinking become impossible. What needs emphasis, however, is that Nabokov notes the prevalence of *poshlust* under conditions of political absolutism not merely because it is an observable and offensive aspect of revolutionary and militant regimes from Stalinist statuary to Mussolinian murals—but because he recognizes in it an indispensable principle of such regimes, a necessary expression of their inner nature.

If we look across from literature to the evidence of history, the gratuitous gestures of the totalitarian state may provide us a clue precisely because they are made out of inner necessity, not from the need to achieve practical ends. Thus, it was the compulsion of their moving spirit, not real utility, that led the Nazis to welcome their unspeakable trainloads of doomed human cattle with brass bands at the railroad sidings blaring cheery patriotic songs. This is totalitarian *poshlust* in the purest form of its moral and aesthetic obscenity; it takes little effort to imagine M'sieur Pierre waving the baton for such a grisly band, a vaguely beery smile playing over his lips. *Poshlust* is indispensable to totalitarianism because it is the natural expression of a deadened consciousness persuaded it is devoted to lofty ends, and at the same time it is the means of foisting sham values, anesthetizing still-human imaginations until they are incapable of making sane distinctions: ugly becomes beautiful, death becomes life, and over the portals of a man-made hell one affixes an ostensibly noble sentiment like *Arbeit macht frei.* "Sentimentality," Norman Mailer has written, "is the emotional promiscuity of those who have no sentiment"; this is why it is in a hideously trashy sentimentalism that the totalitarian spirit comes to full, festering florescence.

There is one passage in *Invitation to a Beheading* that finely illuminates this whole question of the essential, inexorable antagonism between totalitarianism and authentic art. It provides an especially forceful example of how art for Nabokov is inevitably connected with a larger vision of humanity, because here he also deals with the limits of art. We are observing Cincinnatus in his cell once more, though from whose viewpoint we are not informed until the sudden, unsettling turn near the end of the paragraph. Again we are given a portrait composed of precisely selected details—the texture of his skin and hair, the state of his clothing, the movement of his eyes—with abundant indications that these are the details of a carefully executed painting. All these minute particulars, we are told, "completed a picture" that was

made up of a thousand barely noticeable, overlapping trifles: of the light outline of his lips, seemingly not quite fully drawn but touched by a master of masters; of the fluttering movements of his empty, not-yet-shaded-in hands; of the dispersing and again gathering rays in his animated eyes; but even all of this, analyzed and studied, still could not fully explain Cincinnatus: it was as if one side of his being slid into another dimension, as all the complexity of a tree's foliage passes from shade into radiance, so that you cannot distinguish just where begins the submergence into the shimmer of a different element. It seemed as though at any moment, in the course of his movements about the limited space of the haphazardly invented cell, Cincinnatus would step in such a way as to slip naturally and effortlessly through some chink of the air into its unknown coulisses to disappear there with the same easy smoothness with which the reflection of a rotated mirror moves across every object in the room and suddenly vanishes, as if beyond the air, in some new depth of ether. At the same time, everything about him breathed with a delicate, drowsy, but in reality exceptionally strong, ardent and independent life: his veins of the bluest blue pulsated; crystal-clear saliva moistened his lips; the skin quivered on his cheeks and his forehead, which was edged with dissolved light . . . and all this so teased the observer as to make him long to tear apart, cut to shreds, destroy utterly this brazen elusive flesh, and all that it implied and expressed, all that impossible, dazzling freedom—enough, enough— do not walk any more, Cincinnatus, lie down on your cot, so you will not arouse, will not irritate. . . . And in truth Cincinnatus would become aware of the predatory eye in the peephole following him and lie down or sit at the table and open a book. (pp. 121–122)

The opposing attitudes toward human life of the artist and the totalitarian are beautifully dramatized in the contrasted responses to ultimate frustration of the painter's eye at the beginning of the passage and the jailer's eye at the end. Elsewhere in the novel, we have seen how the cunning artist celebrates the power of art to fix reality in arresting pattern; here, however, the narrator confesses the final impotence-in-power of art before the stubborn mystery of an individual human life. In other passages, we noted the use of mirrors as reflecting and perspectival devices that demonstrated the magisterial control of the artist over his materials; here, by contrast, there is no actual mirror in the scene: instead, the mirror is introduced as a simile, a fragment of visual experience used figuratively with paradoxical effectiveness to define the limits of visual representation.

Partial readings of Nabokov's novels have sometimes led to the inference that the world they portray is fundamentally a world of aesthetic solipsism, but this passage makes clear that it is life rather than art alone which is inexhaustible, and that art's ability to renew itself, to be infinitely various and captivating, finally depends upon its necessary inadequacy in the face of the inexhaustible enigma of conscious life. The artist's human subject here glimmers, shimmers, slides into a hidden dimension beyond visualization, but the very frustration of the artist's purpose brings him back to his subject with a sense of loving wonder—all that ardent, independent life pulsing through the bluest of blue veins—the inevitability of partial failure spurring him to attempt again and again the impossible magic of comprehending life in art. With the transition indicated in the text of the novel by the first set of suspension points, the eye at the keyhole changes from the artist-observer's to the jailer's, and immediately the radical elusiveness of the prisoner becomes an infuriating taunt, an outrageous provocation to mayhem. For the artistic consciousness, the two essential activities are wonder and delight; for the totalitarian mentality, the one essential activity is control, manipulation—and therefore mysteries are intolerable, all souls must be "transparent" like the moving parts in a display-motor encased in clear plastic, so that they can at all times be completely accessible to control. Worse than opaque, Cincinnatus is seen here in defiant iridescence, continuing to exercise the inner freedom that his jailers have long since renounced because it was too dizzying, too difficult, interfered in too many complicated ways with the simple, stupefying gratifications of mutual manipulation. One can see why all "freaks," all who are different, must be tortured in this world, and why it is an essential quality of the perfected world of art *là-bas* to leave such creatures wholly unmolested. The peculiarly generalized nature of Cincinnatus as a character serves the purpose of making him function in the novel as an embodiment of the generic possibilities of human freedom.

Although this is a novel about art, it is not, in the conventional sense, a literary portrait of the artist because the artist here is conceived as an everyman, a paradigm of that life of consciousness which is common, at least in potential, to all human beings. Cincinnatus in his cell determines to become a writer not because there is a streak of the aesthete in him but because, finding himself a creature with consciousness in an existence that offers nothing to explain that incredible fact, he envisages art as the fullest, most human response to his own human condition. In the passage we have been considering, Nabokov offers us an external view of the mystery of individual life. Elsewhere, in the pages quoted from Cincinnatus's journal, we get an eloquent statement of that same mystery felt from within. The prisoner contemplates himself issuing from unknowable burning blackness, spinning like a top, headed he knows not where, and he wants desperately to be able to capture in words that crazy, tormenting, somehow stirring condition: "I have no desires, save the desire to express myself—in defiance of all the world's muteness. How frightened I am. How sick with fright. But no one shall take me away from myself" (p. 91). The perspective of *Invitation to a Beheading* is, I think, finally political in Aristotle's sense of the term, not Machiavelli's: by emphasizing an elaborately self-conscious art both as its medium and its moral model, the novel affirms the tough persistence of humanity in a world that is progressively more brutal and more subtle in its attempts to take us away from ourselves.

This essay originally appeared in a special issue of TriQuarterly *devoted to Nabokov on the occasion of his seventieth birthday. Perhaps a bit whimsically, he decided to record a response to each contribution in the next issue of the journal. Most of these were quite* gracious, just a few scolding, George Steiner being an especially egregious target of his disapproval. Here is his brief comment on the essay that is reprinted here:

> Mr. Alter's essay on the "Art of Politics in Invitation to a Beheading" is a most brilliant reflection of that book in a reader's mind. It is practically flawless so that all I can add is that I particularly appreciate his citing a passage from The Gift "that could serve as a useful gloss on the entire nature of political and social reality in the earlier novel."

9

Nabokov and Memory

In Nabokov's notoriously restricted private canon of great twentieth-century novelists—he admitted only Proust, Joyce, Kafka, and Biely—it is Proust who often seems most intimately allied with his own aims and sensibility. A pursuit of time past is undertaken directly or obliquely in many of his novels, and most centrally in what are probably his two finest books— *Lolita* and *Speak, Memory*. The latter is as Proustian as anything Nabokov wrote, and it even includes a little homage to Proust: Nabokov's last vision of Colette, his Riviera childhood sweetheart, rolling a hoop glinting in the autumnal sun through dead leaves in a Parisian park, is a citation, a transposition of pattern from fiction to autobiography, of the scene at the end of *Swann's Way* in which the child Marcel beholds the adored figure of Gilberte Swann playing in the leaves in the Champs-Élysées. The special sense of euphoria associated with the recovery of the sensuous fullness of past experience is equally Nabokov's goal and Proust's, but the routes they follow toward this end notably diverge. The key concept for Proust is of course involuntary memory. The return of the past is vouchsafed by adventitious circumstances as a moment of grace, an unanticipated epiphany. Some otherwise trivial datum of experience, like the wobbling of uneven paving-stones in a Venetian piazza, jogs slumbering memory, flooding consciousness with a complex of seemingly forgotten, perhaps repressed, perceptions from the past. (The articulation of this experience, to be sure, becomes possible only through the finely attuned artistic discipline of the experiencer.) Nabokov, on the other hand, conceives his relation to the past much more exclusively in volitional terms. He is grateful for the occasional mnemonic clues that circumstances may cast his way, but for him the ability to revisit the past is chiefly a consequence of the imaginative concentration afforded by artful prose. It is only a little overstated to say that, for Nabokov, the apt manipulation of language makes the past come back.

A seemingly self-indulgent fantasy in the penultimate paragraph of *Speak, Memory* actually provides a nice definition of the book's project. Nabokov recalls how his four-year-old son, playing on a French Riviera beach not long before their departure for America, would gather tide-tossed treasures from the sea: "candy-like blobs of sea-licked glass—lemon, cherry, peppermint" and "sometimes small bits of pottery, still beautiful in glaze and color." He then reflects on this collection of fragments:

> I do not doubt that among those slightly convex chips of majolica ware found by our child there was one whose border of scrollwork fitted exactly, and continued, the pattern of a fragment I had found in 1903 on the same shore, and that the two tallied with a third my mother had found on that Mentone beach in 1882, and with a fourth piece of the same pottery that had been found by *her* mother a hundred years ago—and so on, until this assortment of parts, if all had been preserved, might have been put together to make the complete, the absolutely complete, bowl, broken by some Italian

child, God knows where and when, and now mended by *these* rivets of bronze.[1]

The meticulous fitting together of fragments into patterns, as Nabokov announces in the opening pages of the book, is what his autobiography is all about. It is at once a task excitingly imaginable and hopelessly impossible, as the language he chooses to evoke the broken bowl suggests. The crucial verbs are in the conditional mode ("if all had been preserved, might have been put together"), implying a condition obviously contrary to fact. The well-wrought urn of the past is, after all, shattered; only a few of its shards can be gathered by the patient memoirist, and that is what is ultimately so wrenching about this remarkably happy autobiography. The "rivets of bronze" that might mend the assembled fragments are of course the fine linkages of Nabokov's polished prose. (The association of bronze with poetic art is confirmed earlier in the book in an explicit reference to Horace's *exegi monumentum*, "I have built a monument more lasting than bronze.") The image of bronze rivets represents precisely the paradoxical character of the undertaking. A majolica bowl put back together with rivets is no longer what it once was, yet it has a new, if patently composite, wholeness, and the bronze that makes this possible, though superimposed on the original substance of the pottery, is itself a burnished material that contributes to an aesthetic effect. The Horatian background of the metaphor also suggests perdurable strength in poetic art, a quality that, as we see, is repeatedly manifested in the stylistic assurance of Nabokov's recuperation of the past.

Humbert Humbert at the beginning of his sad narrative cries out to a forever absent Lolita that he has only words to play with. That is also the desperate situation of the narrator of *Speak,*

Memory vis-à-vis his Russian past, but he is able to overcome absence, to surprise himself with felicity, by refashioning the words into intricate configurations that bring back to him a substantial measure of what he has irrevocably lost. A full explanation of how he achieves this end would involve a comprehensive stylistic analysis of the autobiography. But I think we can get a fair sense of what happens in the prose by concentrating on the means employed to realize one of the most salient aspects of the mnemonic process in the book: the special quality of illumination of the remembered scene.

The equation between light and life—or rather, far more specifically, between life and a crack of light, a limited band of illumination against a large background of darkness—is announced in the very first sentence of *Speak, Memory*, at the beginning of that extraordinary preludic evocation of "chronophobia": "common sense tells us that our existence is but a brief crack of light between two eternities of darkness" (p. 19). This image becomes an organizing motif for the whole autobiography. Having been introduced as a metaphor, it later resurfaces as literal fact in the opening paragraphs of the butterfly chapter:

> On a summer morning, in the legendary Russia of my boyhood, my first glance upon awakening was for the chink between the white inner shutters. If it disclosed a watery pallor, one had better not open them at all, and so be spared the sight of a sullen day sitting for its picture in a puddle. How resentfully one would deduce, from a line of dull light, the leaden sky, the sodden sand, the gruel-like mess of broken brown blossoms under the lilacs—and that flat, fallow leaf (the first casualty of the season) pasted upon a wet garden bench! But if the chink was a long glint of dewy brilliancy,

then I made haste to have the window yield its treasure. With
one blow, the room would be cleft into light and shade. The
foliage of birches moving in the sun had the translucent
green tone of grapes, and in contrast to this there was the
dark velvet of fir trees against a blue of extraordinary intensity, the like of which I rediscovered only many years later, in
the montane zone of Colorado. (p. 119)

The paired scenes—rainy day and sunny day—are actual
recollections of repeated experiences, memory in an iterative
tense, but they also offer themselves as a kind of allegory of
perception and, by implication, of memory. The window (as
often in fiction) is the transparent marker between inner and
outer, between perceiver and scene; and the natural scene as a
whole can be visually reconstructed from the bar of light ema-
nating from it in through the shutters. Nabokov's temporal and
spatial distance from the lost past is defined by that initial
phrase, "the legendary Russia of my boyhood," but the virtuosity of the prose, moving from the chink of light to the nuanced
illumination of the landscape, proceeds to abolish the distance.
The "watery pallor" of the chink of light in the first paragraph
leads the imagination of the observer to a witty image that summarizes the scene he prefers not to behold: "a sullen day sitting
for its picture in a puddle." The wit says a good deal about observation and representation in Nabokov's imaginative world.
It is not merely that the rain puddle reflecting the gloomy sky
is a synecdoche for the whole scene but that framing and mirroring are the means of capturing the fleeting moment. It sometimes seems in Nabokov as though the data of experience were
no more than the raw material of artistic representation, the
majolica shards awaiting the expert hand that will assemble
them in the wholeness of a pattern, and this sense is caught in

the image of the rainy day posing for its picture in the puddle. The idea of a careful photographic composition in grays and dingy browns is then carried forward in the patently composed quality of the prose (quite unlike the paragraph on the sunny day), which locks all the descriptive terms into a network of alliterated *l*'s and *s*'s and *d*'s—"line of dull light," leaden sky," "sodden sand," "gruel-like / lilacs"—complemented by two subseries of *b*'s and *f*'s—"broken brown blossoms," "flat, fallow leaf." None of this can properly be described as onomatopoeic, but the effect is to proffer an illusion of all the words somehow being contaminated by the bleak light of the scene to which they belong, dissolving into one another in a gray impasto, a "gruel-like mess." One begins to see why Nabokov can imagine his prose as bronze rivets, holding pieces firmly together.

The paragraph on the bright day puts aside these artifices of phonetic orchestration partly for contrapuntal reasons, in order not to overdo a single device, and partly because, in this full frontal vision of the illuminated scene, the writer now wants to concentrate on the precise texture of what the light reveals, stressing painterly words instead of mood-evoking sound clusters. The suddenness of the invasion of sunlight when the shutters are flung open is realized in a theatrical gesture, the metaphorical blow that cleaves the room into light and shade. Then we are invited by the chromatic specification of the language to look out the window with the young Vladimir on a visual composition—the delicately defined "translucent green tone of grapes" of the birch leaves set against "the dark velvet" of the fir and the intense blue of the sky. The last of these color values is given neither a tone nor a texture but an emotive label ("extraordinary intensity"); perhaps its location on the spectrum is to be inferred from its relation to the translucent green and the velvet darkness, perhaps because the intensity, confirmed by the rediscovery in Colorado, is the main point. One might note that the Proustian moment of involuntary memory, the unlooked-for recurrence of that sky over Vyra years later in the Rockies, is not the object of representation but an element in the rhetorical structure that fixes the vividness of the primary memory. Nabokov's cunning strangeness with English plays a strategic part in putting this final effect into place. An American would not say "the montane zone" but rather something like "mountain region." The locution, both perfectly correct and oddly foreign, acts to assimilate the mountains of Colorado with the Alps and with Russian topography, just as Nabokov's English in general flaunts its interlinguistic character, makes itself felt as a vehicle that can cross both geographical and temporal boundaries.

Where does the light come from that informs these scenes of memory? The example we have just considered might tempt us into a facile response, namely, that the distinctive quality of light was simply present in the original experience, to be recalled in its peculiar vividness by the lexically fortunate memoirist. Such recollection might follow the Proustian path of consciousness suddenly and happily invaded by the past. For Nabokov, however, the real light that once shone leaves only shadowy traces in the storehouse of memory. It can be recovered not through some spontaneous resurgence but through a careful formal reconstitution in another medium, that of art. It is instructive that light in *Speak, Memory* should be not only a defining presence in remembered scenes but also a recurrent image for art.

In the first chapter, Nabokov, puzzling over the enigma of his own identity, speaks of "a certain intricate watermark whose unique design becomes visible when the lamp of art is made to shine through life's foolscap" (p. 25). This image of art as the illuminator of otherwise hidden patterns dovetails with the repeated representation of memory in the figure of the magic lantern, as Nabokov notes that the sundry tutors of his boyhood "appear within memory's luminous disc as so many magic-lantern projections." A magic lantern, by putting light behind a colored transparency, transforms it into a larger illuminated image that, even in its necessary two-dimensionality, may seem enchantingly lifelike. (One recalls the prominence of the magic lantern in Proust.) Let us look briefly at a few selected slides from *Speak, Memory* to see how Nabokov performs this trick by a delicate positioning of the lamp of his art.

One of the oddest images conjured up in the autobiography is the view from the dining room at the Vyra manor of Nabokov's father being tossed in a blanket outside by his servants. It is not sufficient to pigeonhole this moment as an instance of the technique of defamiliarization of which Nabokov was past master, because the arabesque movement of the prose also leads to a perception of the intimate and paradoxical liaison between presence and absence, life and death, reality and art:

> Thrice, to the mighty heave-ho of his invisible tossers, he would fly up in this fashion, and the second time he would go higher than the first and then there he would be, on his last and loftiest flight, reclining, as if for good, against the cobalt blue of the summer noon, like one of those paradisiac personages who comfortably soar, with such a wealth of folds in their garments, on the vaulted ceiling of a church while below, one by one, the wax tapers in mortal hands light up to make a swarm of minute flames of incense, and the priest chants of eternal repose, and funeral lilies conceal the face of whoever lies there, among the swimming lights, in the open coffin. (pp. 31–32)

Nabokov's prose often has the look of working out carefully calculated effects, but here, one may venture to guess, he seems to have given himself over to the free-associative momentum of metaphor, with startling consequences. The narration of the father tossed in a blanket by boisterous peasants ends—it is also the chapter ending—in a kind of freeze-frame that stresses the timeless thereness ("there would be") of the horizontal figure "reclining" against the summer sky "as if for good." Father, day, and year are all at a lofty still point (it is noon, and close to the summer solstice).

Characteristically, Nabokov realizes this moment in part through recourse to a painterly term, "the cobalt blue of the summer noon." This immediately leads associatively to the elaborate simile of the painted image of the divine or saintly figures on the church ceiling. That simile is "Homeric" not merely in its length but in its power to effect a large movement between two disparate realms. The living image of the father in midair is transposed into painting on plaster, the painted figures linked with a more ecclesiastic paradise than the boy experienced in his childhood world. In a macabre turn of wit, the wonderful suspension on air turns into the "eternal repose" of the priestly chant, and, with the rightness of dream logic, the dead person's face is concealed. As the perspective moves from life to iconography and from outside to inside, the lighting appropriately switches from solar brilliance to flickering wax tapers that cast their faint gleam, as we spiral down through the last clause from ceiling to ground, onto an open coffin.

This concluding image of a body recumbent in death does not, I think, subvert or cancel the image of a splendidly living body recumbent in air, as one school of contemporary criticism would automatically conclude. What it seems to me rather to do is to add a dimension of terrible poignancy to the captured timeless moment of the soaring father. As surely as the memoirist is aware that his father was cut down by an assassin's bullet in 1922, he knows, and his figurative language dramatizes visually, that the cobalt blue of the remembered sky is drawn against a shadowy background of extinction—precisely like the crack of light at the beginning of the book set between two eternities of darkness.

Memories of a happy, forever-lost childhood can easily decline into the cheap coin of nostalgia. What partly makes *Speak, Memory* one of the most remarkable of modern autobiographies is Nabokov's ability to convey in prose the precious vividness of his past while keeping steadily in mind the necessary fate it shares with every human past of being swallowed up by oblivion. Only the intervention of art grants it the grace of a radiant afterlife, but that is, ineluctably, different in kind from the first life. Instructively, at the end of chapter 3, Nabokov fleetingly evokes an infinite regress of adults remembering childhood. Rereading the sentimental juvenile fiction of a certain Mme de Ségur, née Rostopchine, he relives his own boyhood when he first read these books, and in a painful doubling, he remembers his Uncle Ruka reading Mme de Ségur back in 1908 and reliving *his* boyhood:

> I see again my schoolroom in Vyra, the blue roses of the wallpaper, the open window. Its reflection fills the oval mirror above the leathern couch where my uncle sits, gloating over a tattered book. A sense of security, of well-being, of summer warmth pervades my memory. That robust reality makes a ghost of the present. The mirror brims with brightness; a

bumblebee has entered the room and bumps against the ceiling. Everything is as it should be, nothing will ever change,
nobody will ever die. (p. 77)

Again, a window, light from the outside, and a mirror—this last,
a Nabokov trademark—make the scene cohere. As in our previous illustration, the power of the memory is brought out in a
play between presence and absence, life and death, but the rhetorical balance here is quite different. The sheer happiness of
the remembered experience is explicitly announced, and the
memoirist goes as far as to reverse the categories of presence
and absence: "That robust reality makes a ghost the present."
The robustness is mysteriously reinforced by the alliterated r's,
while the assimilation through near-rhyme of "robust" and
"ghost" draws us into a somewhat disorienting semantic shell
game: it is the past, after all, that is a ghost, but a robust one that
makes what we usually call reality seem spectral. The final focus
on the paired images of the sun-flooded mirror and the bumblebee is articulated with a Tennysonian musicality, emphatically
clustering m's and b's and r's in a pattern of sound that turns
into an onomatopoeic evocation of the buzzing, bumping bumblebee. The more important effect, however, of the phonetic
interfusion of words in this penultimate sentence is to convey
in the bronze rivets of prose a sense of all the elements of an
experienced moment beautifully, timelessly locked together.
But the last sentence—"Everything is as it should be, nothing
will ever change, nobody will ever die"—is disquietingly
double-edged. It hovers precariously between a rapturous proclamation and an anguished *cri de coeur*. On one level, it is a true
declaration—on the level that every reader can experience in
the stylistic success of an undying memory crystallized in

language that makes the wallpaper, the uncle, the book, and the mirror brimming with brightness live on. But both narrator and reader are also acutely aware that the final sentence is flagrantly contrary to existential fact: each of its affirmations is necessarily shadowed by a negation, for nothing remains as it should be, everything always changes, everyone dies.

The more one ponders this enchanting book, the more evident it becomes that Nabokov's conception of memory is profoundly—and appropriately—ambiguous. In the same breath, he intimates that he has recovered or somehow reconstituted the past in his prose and that he has reinvented a past forever lost in the vanishing perspective of time. To affirm merely the former would be to succumb to self-indulgent delusion; to affirm merely the latter would be to concede that autobiography is impossible because it must always turn into fiction. He defines "the supreme achievement of memory" as "the masterly use it makes of innate harmonies when gathering to its fold the suspended and wandering tonalities of the past." The adjective "innate" here hovers indeterminately. The structure of experience may involve innate harmonies, as Nabokov seems to propose in his sundry remarks on pattern. Alternately, there may be an aesthetic order, distinct from experience as such, that has its intrinsic harmonies—the consonance of images, the pleasing recurrences of sound—and these may be exploited by artful consciousness to pull together the disparate fragments of experience. He tends toward the first alternative, which makes the act of autobiographical recovery a triumphant reality, but he repeatedly allows for the second alternative as well, in which autobiography is perforce an artifice offering a kind of luminous compensation for the unrecoverable past.

Nabokov's evocation of the initial trip of his Swiss governess, "Madamoiselle," from the rural train station to the family estate vividly illustrates this delicate ambiguity. It contains features shared by most of the examples we have considered—an emphatically defined source of illumination, mirror imagery, painterly elements of composition—and provides a nice nocturnal complement to the sunlit scenes we have looked at:

> Every now and then, she looks back to make sure that a second sleigh, bearing her trunk and hatbox, is following—always at the same distance, like those companionable phantoms of ships in polar waters which explorers have described. And let me not leave out the moon—for surely there must be a moon, the full, incredibly clear disc that goes so well with Russian lusty frosts. So there it comes, steering out of a flock of small dappled clouds, which it tinges with a vague iridescence; and, as it sails higher, it glazes the runner tracks left on the road, where every sparkling lump of snow is emphasized by a swollen shadow. Very lovely, very lonesome. But what am I doing in this stereoscopic dreamland? How did I get here? Somehow, the two sleighs have slipped away, leaving behind a passportless spy standing on the blue-white road in his New England snowboots and stormcoat. The vibration in my ears is no longer their receding bells, but only my own blood singing. All is still, spellbound, enthralled by the moon, fancy's rear-vision mirror. The snow is real, though, and as I bend to it and scoop up a handful, sixty years crumble to glittering frost-dust between my fingers. (pp. 99–100)

In this instance, the status of the recalled scene as sheer invention is flaunted from the start. In actuality, the child Vladimir was back at the Vyra manor when this moonlit ride took place, and so Nabokov the memoirist must re-create it as a fiction writer from Mademoiselle's point of view, to a large extent using the clues of literary convention. The following sleigh is wittily represented as a counterpart to those "companionable phantoms of ships" sighted by polar explorers, and the shimmer of oscillation between phantom or hallucination and real thing runs through the whole scene. The moon cannot be left out, the narrator ostentatiously announces, and it is thus introduced with suitable theatricality ("So there it comes"), providing iridescence for the clouds, glitter and melodramatic shadows for the snow.

This magical landscape collapses with the interjection, "Very lovely, very lonesome." It has all been a "stereoscopic dreamland," a term that suggests still another guide of artifice for the composition of the scene—the old stereoscopes with their "picturesque" black-and-white views showing two dimensions as three that were a common home amusement in the world of Nabokov's childhood. The Russia of 1906, in a kind of cinematic *faux raccord* (the opposite of a Proustian concordance), disappears into a New England winterscape decades later in which the expatriate writer, "a passportless spy" on the remembered Mademoiselle, is equally exiled from his homeland and his past. But even here, the act of imaginative recollection is dialectic. The New England moon is "fancy's rear-vision mirror." As the chronophobic, chronophiliac imagination looks "back" into it, the moon becomes the moon of 1906, no mere mechanism of *faux raccord*, and, in the last emblematic gesture, sixty years crumble to frost-dust as dreamworld and real world change places.

The obtruded paradox of this extreme instance is submerged but implicit in most of the evoked scenes of *Speak, Memory*. The memory of Mademoiselle's sleigh ride is an invention, directed by the principles of internal coherence and mimetic aptness of literary, painterly, and perhaps photographic artifice. And yet artifice, whether dealing with past or present, is our principal means of crystallizing experience, making it emotionally and aesthetically assimilable precisely by playing up those "innate harmonies." The moon is a literary stage prop and still the real moon seen by a wide-eyed child in the winter sky over Vyra in 1906, just as the chill touch of snow is real, then and now.

Few imaginative writers have been so committed as Nabokov to the ideal of conscious control. In his autobiography he often evinces a sense that he can actually stage a return to the past by a sufficiently deft and resourceful ordering of his prose medium. But there is also an aspect of Proustian involuntarism stalking this project of artful volition. The scene of memory invoked, whether actual recollection or invention or a subtle compound of the two, picks up an experiential charge from the present, sets up a circulation between past and present that is not strictly determined by artistic calculation.

This, indeed, is why *Speak, Memory* is not simply a series of virtuoso tricks in constructing the past but a haunting expression of what it means to live in time, circling back on the past, intimately bound to it, yet also forever exiled in another, later world. Nabokov's folding together of past and present is thus more than just an autobiographical gesture—his own story, so plangently told here, becomes an articulation of how everyone lives in time, exiled from the past, possessed by it, striving to recover it through a sustained effort of the imagination. In this way, *Speak, Memory*, surely Nabokov's most intensely personal book, is also the luminous evocation of a universal human experience.

10

Lectures on Literature

Vladimir Nabokov, according to the published testimony of several of his students at Cornell during the 1950s, was an extraordinary teacher—unorthodox in his methods, alternately beguiling and amusing in his manner, and above all compelling in the vision of literary art he conveyed to his classes. Nabokov's striking success as a teacher might in itself raise questions about the quality of relentlessly self-admiring aloofness that certain critics have attributed to him. Few full-time writers make good teachers (Nabokov's friend of those years, Edmund Wilson, who refused to do any teaching, is an apposite case in point) for the obvious and understandable reason that they are too wrapped up in their own writing to exercise much attentiveness to the special intellectual needs and deficiencies of the young. Nabokov, however, once exile and poverty had cast him unexpectedly onto the lecturer's podium, was able to kindle his students with the carefully written lecture texts he read out to them because, for all his witty playfulness, he felt—if I may use an appropriately old-fashioned phrase—a moral passion about what he was teaching. He was also something of a performer, which is not true of many writers, and the available reports suggest that he enjoyed performing before the audiences in a large lecture hall. In any case, his Cornell lectures offer a window into his ideas about the nature and purpose of fiction.

During the last years of his life, Nabokov intimated several times that he intended to prepare for publication these lectures on modern fiction. After the appearance of the first volume of them appeared in 1980—a second, devoted solely to Russian writers, would be published the following year—one readily sees the practical difficulty that must have made Nabokov hesitate about reworking his Cornell material. These are very much classroom lectures rather than critical essays, complete with illustrations of Nabokov's pedagogic diagrams and drawings in the scrupulous edition by Fredson Bowers from the author's holograph.[1] Though Nabokov affirms an overriding interest in style and structure, and occasionally has instructive perceptions to share on these matters of form, his mode of exposition is by and large demonstrative rather than analytic. He proceeds on the assumption, no doubt warranted for the students of Literature 311–312, that his audience is made up of innocent readers going, or perhaps stumbling, through the books under consideration for the first time.

His principal strategy, then, for explaining *Mansfield Park, Madame Bovary,* "The Metamorphosis," *Ulysses,* and other works is to retell the story of each in considerable detail, with frequent quotations of lengthy passages, often followed by the simple comment that the passage just read is "wonderfully artistic." Sustained by Nabokov's vivid personal presence and his distinctive style of oral delivery, this method, as John Updike observes in his engaging introduction, could have a thoroughly magnetic effect, but on the printed page the synopses, however gracefully written, are still synopses, and the quotations are, alas, no more than quotations. The limitations of such a mode of presentation are perhaps most evident in the lecture on

Proust, a writer Nabokov loved dearly, and whom he saw as a model of what might be achieved through the art of literature. Apart from a few nice observations on Proust's style and in particular on his use of metaphor, the lecture is a series of passages from the novel, with bridges of paraphrase by the lecturer from one large island of quotation to the next.

There are, I should add, some illuminating perceptions in the lectures, illuminating even for the experienced reader. Nabokov of course views these novelists with the canny eye of a fellow craftsman, and at times he is acute in seeing how things are put together, how the writer leads up to a particular scene, synchronizes and intermeshes different subplots and groups of characters, announces a theme and then cunningly weaves it in and out of the fabric of his fiction. Thus, it is Nabokov's practical feeling for the difficulties of assembling a complex fictional structure that brings him to the shrewd detection of what he calls the "layers" theme in *Madame Bovary*, beginning with young Charles's grotesquely layered cap in the opening scene, resurfacing in Charles's and Emma's layered wedding cake, then in the elaborately described tiers of their house at Toste, and concluding wryly in the triple-tiered construction of Emma's coffin.

This attention to the nuts-and-bolts aspects of great novels is combined with an exquisitely tuned sensibility that sometimes, even in the inertness of the printed page, justifies the demonstrative method. That is, in some instances the illustrative passages are so perfectly chosen, the brief commentary on them so apt, that one gets a renewed and refined sense of the particular novel's special magic, as when Nabokov shows us a magisterial description in *Bleak House* of the fog rising like a curtain above the Thames to reveal a sun shining through clouds and "making silvery pools in the dark sea," which bustles with the

motion of ships coming and going. Nabokov quotes a paragraph of the description, then comments for another paragraph
on the visual precision, the musical felicity of what he has
quoted, and on the place of the scene in the artistic economy of
the novel. It is a lovely exercise of critical tact, and it communi-
cates, as more conventionally academic analyses might not, the
sheer pleasure of reading.

In any case, what chiefly makes *Lectures on Literature* a book
to be cherished, despite its *longueurs* of summary and citation,
is the moving sense it conveys of what great fiction is for. Nabokov articulates here not a poetics but a metaphysics of fiction.
The writer, he repeatedly proclaims, is above all else an en-
chanter. This insistence has a certain polemical edge, cutting
against the stolidly representational function ascribed to the
novel—"the epic of bourgeois society"—by most critical
schools until the advent of French structuralism. But if Nabokov rejects simple representational views of the novel, shrewdly
showing how even supposedly realistic novels casually flout the
laws of quotidian reality or invent their own laws, he does not
move in the direction many readers might expect, toward the
notion of the self-referentiality of the literary text that was so
fashionable among followers in the academy of the *nouvelle critique.* There is, as he sees it, a definite relation between fiction
and reality, but it is not so much reflective or mimetic as consti-
tutive. This is the ultimate justification of his conceiving the
artist as magician: the magician is someone who at once performs tricks by sleight of hand and calls things into being, conjures them up seemingly out of thin air.

An antithetical image of bad writing may make clearer what
lies behind this notion of fiction and reality. It occurs as part of
a protest against didactic and documentary fiction in a compact
essay, "The Art of Literature and Commonsense," which serves

here as a concluding lecture and is the one perfect gem of the volume. Nabokov observes:

> The writer's pulpit is dangerously close to the pulp romance and what reviewers call a strong novel is generally a precarious heap of platitudes or a sand castle on a populated beach, and there are few things sadder than to see its muddy moat dissolve when the holiday makers are gone and the cold mousy waves are nibbling at the solitary sands. (p. 376)

The brilliance of the wit, the elegant interlocking of alliterative sound and cadence in order to realize the figurative scene, of course constitute a counterexample of something made out of words that will stand a while in time, but I should like to call attention in particular to what is implied by the imagery. Reality, Nabokov avers at a number of points with a flourish of philosophical subjectivism, is what each of us makes of it in the darkroom of his mind. The average mind, however, being lazy or fearful or both, prefers to work with stock concepts, prefabricated notions shared by multitudes, and it is to this tacit conspiracy of intellectual sloth or cowardice that the popularity of popular literature, from the cheapest sentimental fiction and pornography to the bogus idealism of middlebrow *poshlust*, can be traced. The producers of such literature not only build on sand but, childlike, with sand, slapping together what comes to hand; and their work, lacking the strong cement of imagination, is no more than seeming structure, doomed in a moment to slide back into formlessness.

Those mousy nibbling waves at the end of Nabokov's vignette suggest what, in his view, the serious writer is faced with. The sea is ultimately an image of chaos, and chaos is an active, menacing presence, undercutting every moment we breathe with impermanence and the negation of meaning. Chaos is invoked explicitly at the beginning of the introductory lecture in a most Nabokovian refashioning of Genesis 1:

> The material of this world may be real enough (as far as reality goes) but does not exist at all as an accepted entirety: it is chaos and to this chaos the author says "go!" allowing the world to flicker and to fuse. It is now recombined in its very atoms, not merely in its visible and superficial parts. (p. 2)

The writer does not settle for fragments and random particles, building sandcastles, but, on the contrary, makes his own whole out of the jumbled elements of experience; so the aim of his enterprise is not to recover reality but to achieve it.

There is a complicated paradox here that can be fully understood only by following Nabokov's readings of particular novels, and especially of *Bleak House* (in several respects the best of the lectures). On one hand, he insists on the primacy of fantasy in constituting the work of fiction; on the other hand, he clearly does not assume that any old fantasy will do, that the writer's power to make worlds out of words is absolutely arbitrary. Despite the affirmed rejection of a real world outside of literature and the mind, he evinces a certain underlying commitment to it, as I have contended in all these essays. The effect of a great work of literature, he proposes with an instructive switch of expected epithets he also uses elsewhere, is "the Precision of Poetry and the Excitement of Science." Both the precision and the excitement, I think, point simultaneously to the fashioning of the artwork itself and to the materials of the world out of which it was fashioned. That is, the excitement is obviously the excitement of discovery, but this is both the discovery of the cunning interrelation of parts in the work (like the recurrence of layered things in *Madame Bovary*) and the discovery within the work of something perfectly seen that we may have glimpsed briefly and badly in our extraliterary experience. Similarly, poetry is precise both because of the exquisite internal adjustment of its minute parts and because it uses just the right word, sound, rhythm, image to catch the desired nuance of feeling, visual value, moral relation, or whatever the case may be. If for Nabokov there can be no accepted reality for the writer to represent, literature nevertheless constantly deals with realities, focusing them, crystallizing them, giving them permanence through its power of artistic definition, which might be succinctly characterized as the architectonic exercise of bold fantasy sustained by close observation.

One decisive element needs to be added to this picture of Nabokov's metaphysics of fiction, and that is time. It's no wonder that he became a writer preoccupied with the poignancy and urgency of time, given the temporal cataclysm through which he lived: the whole world in which he grew up had been swept away irrevocably by the Russian Revolution at the moment he was entering manhood. We are all trapped by time, Nabokov came to feel, we are all time's victims, unless we can find a way to prevail against it through art. The rodent sea, nibbling away fragile structures—one thinks of the remembered beach idyll in *Speak, Memory* and of its transmutation in *Lolita*—might also be an image of *tempus edax*, time the devourer of human things. Thus memory is an important component in the process of artistic creation as Nabokov describes it (and Proust is an exemplary figure for him), but it is memory dynamically interacting with unconscious feeling, with lucid perception of the present, and with the ordering sense that produces coherent artistic form. The writer does not recapture the past but rather incorporates it into the transcendence of time's terrible flux, which he experiences through his writing: "It is the

past and the present and the future (your book) that come together with a sudden flash; thus the entire circle of time is perceived, which is another way of saying that time ceases to exist"
(p. 378). This special dynamic of the writer's deployment of
memory is spectacularly visible in *Speak, Memory*.

Interestingly, these climactic moments of creation engender
in Nabokov not a feeling of godlike elevation but an almost
mystic sense of merging with the world outside himself:

> It is a combined sensation of having the whole universe enter-
> ing you and of yourself wholly dissolving in the universe
> around you. It is the prison wall of the ego suddenly crum-
> bling away with the non-ego rushing in from the outside to
> save the prisoner—who is already dancing in the open.
> (p. 378)

With all this in mind, we may better understand why Nabokov took his lectureship as an urgent occasion for demonstrating to students the supreme importance of literary art, and why
he associated art not only with lucidity and harmony but also
with compassion and—he does not shrink from the word—
goodness. Art is one's articulate refusal to acquiesce in the overriding reality of chaos, whether chaos is embodied in the blind
rush of time, the imbecilities of mass culture, or the murderous
reign of totalitarian states. It is that vision of art realized in fiction which accounts for the underlying moral seriousness,
amidst all the stratagems and games, of *The Gift, Invitation to a
Beheading, Lolita,* and *Pale Fire,* and makes them deserve to
stand with the enduring achievements of the novel.

Nabokov's moral seriousness in thinking about the novel is
illuminated in an odd but instructive way in *Lectures on Literature* in the chapter on Dickens's *Bleak House.* One might perhaps think that Dickens should be precisely the sort of writer

toward whom Nabokov would direct his customary disdainful dismissal. The two are antithetical in certain obvious ways. Dickens wrote at breakneck speed for serial publication whereas Nabokov claimed to have rewritten every sentence of his novels several times. In contrast to the Flaubertian model admired by Nabokov of the novel as an exquisitely wrought artifice, Dickens typically proceeded in a virtually slapdash manner, trotting out all the tricks of popular and even sensationalist fiction— elaborate contrivances of plot, often depending on improbable coincidence, patently concocted suspense, moralizing that could verge on preaching, blandness in most of the "good" characters, and a sentimentality that has often been duly excoriated by his critics. Nabokov recognizes all of these in his discussion of *Bleak House*, noting them as failings of the novel and at one point even confessing, for example, that, for his part, he would never have allowed the unswervingly virtuous Esther to act as a narrator. And yet *Bleak House* is among the novels in *Lectures on Literature* for which Nabokov expresses the keenest enthusiasm.

The reasons for his perhaps surprising admiration of Dickens are worth exploring. Much of Nabokov's enthusiasm, understandably, is inspired by Dickens's spectacular use of figurative language. As a few critics have observed, Dickens is probably the greatest master of metaphor in the English language after Shakespeare. His metaphors and similes gush forth in a seemingly inexhaustible stream, figurative comparisons that are very often quite unexpected, sometimes wild and fantastic, but in most cases serving as little epiphanies of character, plot, and theme. Thus the novel's bravura evocation of London fog in its opening page has often been celebrated, but I think no one has noticed so keenly as Nabokov the interfusion between fog and mud and its multifarious ramifications, fraught with thematic significance, throughout the novel. He aptly characterizes this interfusion:

> Accumulating at compound interest, [Dickens's metaphor] links the real mud and mist to the mud and muddle of Chancery. Sitting in the midst of the mist and the mud and the muddle, the Lord Chancellor is addressed by Mr. Tagle as "Mlud." At the heart of the mud and fog, "My Lord" is himself reduced to "Mud" if we remove the lawyer's slight lisp. My Lord, Mlud, mud. We shall mark at once, at the very beginning of our inquiry, that this is a typical Dickensian device of wordplay, making inanimate words not only live but perform tricks transcending their immediate sense. (p. 72)

Nabokov, who loved to play with the sound of words and was especially enamored of alliteration, is acutely responsive to Dickensian sound-play, even if its practice in *Bleak House* is rather different from his own. And, of course, he introduces his own sound play into his interpretive comment—"in the midst of the mist and the mud and the muddle"—riffing on Dickens.

What Nabokov sees in Dickens's figurative language, especially at its most fantastic, is that it is both immensely entertaining and revelatory, which is clearly what he thinks the sundry aspects of a good novel should be. Here is a brief passage on Krook that he admires:

> He was short, cadaverous, and withered; with his head sunk sideways between his shoulders, and the breath issuing in visible smoke from his mouth, as if he were on fire within. His throat, chin, and eyebrows were so frosted with white hairs, and so gnarled with veins and puckered skin, that he

looked from his breast upward, like some old root in a fall of snow. (p. 77)

The obvious thing about this description is the smoke and fire that presage Krook's bizarre death by spontaneous combustion. But there is more here. Krook's "cadaverous, and withered look," head tilted sideways and sunk between his shoulders, gives him the appearance of a walking corpse, perhaps a hanged man upon whom a verdict of capital punishment issued by the court has been carried out. Dickens, moreover, does not hesitate to compound simile upon simile as he takes us from the cadaver burning inwardly to the gnarled root breaking out of the snow-covered ground. The passage constitutes a brilliant, thematically pointed riot of figurative invention, which is one of the reasons, in Nabokov's view, that we read novels.

The metaphorical image, he suggests, invites us to reflect and at the same time *to see.* Thus, he observes of a phrase about a heavily burning, rapidly melting candle ("a great cabbage head and a long winding-sheet") with a didactic admonition to his student audience, "No use reading Dickens if one cannot visualize that" (pp. 78–79). In keeping with the metaphor just cited, the Dickens lecture offers a small anthology of piquant and unforgettable metaphors. The egregious Mrs. Jellyby's unkempt hair looks "like the mane of a dustman's horse" (p. 117). (To the American reader: a dustman is a garbage collector.) Of the church at the Dedlocks' estate, it is said, "the oaken pulpit breaks out in a cold sweat; and there is a general smell and taste as of the ancient Dedlocks in their graves" (p. 115). A lamplighter extinguishing the gas streetlamps at dawn "going his rounds, like an executioner to a despotic king, strikes off the little heads of fire that have aspired to lessen the darkness" (p. 118). A lugubrious attorney, "Mr. Vholes, quiet and unmoved, as a man of so much respectability ought to be, takes off his close black gloves as if he were skinning his hands, lifts off his tight hat as if he were scalping himself, and sits down at his desk" (p. 118). A walk-on character is represented as "a short, shrewd niece, something too violently compressed about the waist, and with a sharp nose like a sharp autumn evening, inclining to be frosty towards the end" (p. 122).

Sometimes, this play of figuration is chiefly Dickens being exuberantly Dickensian for the purposes of momentary amusement, as would appear to be the case with the sharp-nosed niece. What is remarkable—and Nabokov duly remarks on it— is how often these fantastic figures interconnect and further our imaginative perception as readers of what is going on in the novel. It should be observed, just in the small sample I have offered here, how often these images suggest death and decay or life being choked out by something deathlike, or they become something ghoulish, as in the representation of Mr. Vholes. Early in the nineteenth century, Coleridge coined from the Greek a somewhat rebarbative but useful term that for obvious reasons has not entered general usage: "esemplastic." It is defined in the *Oxford English Dictionary* as "molding into unity." For Nabokov, this is an essential feature of any great novel and perhaps why he never worked up much enthusiasm for the amicably ambling *Don Quixote*. His own procedure for molding the disparate parts of a long fiction into unity was quite different from that of Dickens. From what we can infer, it was carefully, cunningly calibrated and then worked out through the writing in minute detail as Nabokov shuffled and reshuffled those five-by-eight cards on which he wrote. One might cite the squirrels in *Pnin* or the mirrors in *Pale Fire*, to which detailed attention is given elsewhere in this book. Dickens seems to have achieved this end through intuitively driven improvisation, perhaps not always fully conscious of the web he was weaving. In any case, Nabokov admired the unity Dickens had achieved, and in his exposition of *Bleak House* for the benefit of his students he repeatedly points to the interlinked images and traces the development of major themes in the novel, even using diagrams that twine the themes together.

There is another aspect of this novel that Nabokov highlights, one likely to surprise some of his readers. To invoke a term rarely encountered in literary criticism, it is compassion. His emphasis on this idea tells us something about one of the purposes he thought novels should serve. He of course concedes that at moments Dickens can be lamentably sentimental, but he argues that in much of the novel something quite different is happening: "Dickens's great art should not be mistaken for a cockney version of the seat of emotion—it is the real thing, keen, subtle, specialized compassion, with a grading and merging of melting shades, with the very accent of profound pity in the words uttered, and with an artist's choice of the most visible, most audible, most tangible epithets" (p. 87). In this connection, he cites in particular the treatment of victimized children in the novel—most prominently, the sad little street sweeper Jo, who will die of smallpox; the children of Mrs. Jellyby, who become the hapless victims of their scandalously neglectful mother; and there are others. Nabokov's own novels are often thought of as elaborately inventive games of chess with the reader, perhaps excessively ingenious and rather too cerebral. But compassion figures in them more importantly than is often noticed. Fiction for Nabokov is not just a game but an instrument for evoking the plight of the helpless, a vividly realized prod to the moral imagination. One might think of John Shade's sad daughter in *Pale Fire*, who ends as a suicide;

the inveterately bumbling Pnin, a loving man repeatedly confronted with rejection, whose wife has betrayed him with the heartless narrator; and, above all, Lolita, robbed of her childhood to satisfy Humbert Humbert's sexual perversion.

Nabokov was an intensely visual novelist, and I have already cited an instance where he emphasizes *seeing* what Dickens has imagined. There is an underlying link between his praise of compassion as a novelistic virtue and the striking visuality that he celebrates in Dickens. Alongside the fantastic grotesquery of many of Dickens's metaphoric inventions, he is—as Nabokov, but few others, notes—a fine observer in his descriptions of places, houses, and, above all, urban scenes. Nabokov expresses particular admiration for the scene mentioned above, a rendering of the London harbor, the sun on the Thames as it comes through the clouds "making silvery pools in the dark sea." For the reader, Nabokov proposes, this should elicit a "thrill of recognition," for it is "something Dickens noted for the very first time with the innocent and sensuous eye of the true artist" (p. 116).

What does this have to do with the novelistic moral value of compassion? Nabokov repeatedly proclaims his abhorrence of generalities—in fiction and in literary history and criticism, and he emphatically states this disapproval in *Lectures on Literature*. It is the task of the novelist, he argues, to make us see the individual situation, setting, event, or character in all its particularity. This is what he has in mind when he speaks here and elsewhere of "the precision of poetry." The Thames in sunlight peeking through clouds is a place and moment realized in the nuance and concreteness of its particular manifestation with the fine perceptiveness of the novelist's eye. I think Nabokov means to suggest that what is true of scene is equally true of character. What redeems little Jo from sentimental bathos is that he is not a generic London street urchin but a poor waif with an individual history and, even in his wholly untutored way, with an individual sense of the world. The inarticulateness through which he struggles to express what he has seen, his gratitude toward those who have been kind to him in his cruel circumstances, are distinctively his, and so the compassion we are expected to feel for him has been earned by the novelist. The drive to precision in the writing of fiction, which in Nabokov's view should impel every good writer, in this way carries with it a moral imperative.

It should be noted, however, that the particularizing imagination of the novelist operates pervasively and is not limited to fleshing out large themes or realizing individual character. As Nabokov sees it, the writer's attention to minute detail is part of the reader's sheer pleasure in the novel. At the very end of the lecture on Dickens, he offers a piquant example. Dickens describes a person flashing on to the scene of the novel for only a moment, a man who ekes out a meager living by holding horses and hailing coaches, for which service he is paid very small change. This figure, dressed in "an old red jacket," here "receives his twopence with anything but transport, tosses the money into the air, catches it over-handed and retires." None of this serves any larger purpose of the book, but Nabokov, with the admiring eye of a fellow writer, sees its vivid effect: "This gesture, this one gesture, with its epithet 'over-handed'—a trifle—but the man is alive forever in a good reader's mind." He goes on to conclude that the world a writer creates is "a magic democracy" where even the most incidental character "has the right to live and breathe" (p. 124). Despite Nabokov's peremptory dismissal of so many writers, this is a capacious, open-ended view of the novel.

His own fiction abounds in moments where a transient character, a building, a moving van, an American motel, all sorts of things, leap to life as they are freshly and carefully perceived. One may recall the bespectacled railroad conductor in the first chapter of *Pnin;* the "round-backed Tartar" observed from a window in Saxony in *Despair,* "in an embroidered skullcap . . . showing a small red carpet to a buxom, barefooted woman"; in that same novel, the French mistress of a Berlin dentist presiding over his waiting room, "seated at her desk among vials of blood-red Lawson mouthwash," pursing her lips as she "nervously scratche[s] her scalp"; chairs being moved in a Russian church in *The Defense* "with the sound of throats being cleared" (this last, rather Dickensian). The examples are endless. All these bear witness to Nabokov's sense of the novel as a form that requires exacting craft, close observation, and a constant imagination of concrete things. His Cornell lectures stand on some perhaps ambiguous middle ground between pedagogic demonstrations for undergraduates of the power of fiction and perceptive literary criticism, but they abundantly demonstrate his notion of fiction as a species of magic engaging reality that is repeatedly manifested in his novels. The fact, moreover, that he can celebrate writers as different from himself and from each other as Austen, Kafka, and Proust reflects a receptivity to the many varieties of fiction that his more dogmatic pronouncements might not lead one to expect.

Perhaps what finally links the various writers he admires is a quality of grasping things whole through an intuition of imagination, however disparate the fragments, which Nabokov finds in all of them. "The Art of Literature and Commonsense," his fascinating essay appended to *Lectures on Literature,* affords insight into this conception of the act of writing, emphatically evoked from a writer's point of view. Just before the conclusion of the essay, he offers the following image of the writer launching on his or her novel:

> The pages are still blank, but there is a miraculous feeling of the words all being there, written in invisible ink and clamoring to become visible. You might if you choose develop any part of the picture, for the idea of sequence does not really exist as far as the author is concerned. Sequence arises only because words have to be written one after the other on consecutive pages, just as the reader's mind must have time to go through the book, at least the first time he reads it. Time and sequence cannot exist in the author's mind because no time element and no space element had ruled the initial vision. If the mind were constructed on optional lines and if a book could be read in the same way as a painting is taken in by the eye, that is without the bother of working from left to right and without the absurdity of beginnings and ends, this would be the ideal way of appreciating a novel, for thus the author saw it at the moment of its conception. (pp. 379–380)

It seems quite likely that many novelists do not view their work in this way, but the idea of the writer operating beyond the limits of time and space tells us something about how Nabokov approached novel-writing, an approach manifested in his composing on index cards that did not have a necessary set sequence. It also points forward to his metaphysically unsatisfactory experiment, late in his career, in reversing or abolishing time in *Ada*. If good fiction dismisses the world of common sense with all its platitudes, as his essay argues, it is in large part because the writer has a gift for pushing beyond the hobbling limitations of time and space that encourage us to see only one thing after another, one thing distinct and separate from every other thing. The unities of plot and theme and metaphor and motif, as they are variously practiced in *Madame Bovary, Mansfield Park, Dr. Jekyll and Mr. Hyde,* and *Ulysses,* rebuild the world in integrated revelatory coherences. Ultimately, that may be what Nabokov means in his repeated insistence on the magic of literature.

11

Style in the Novel, Style in Nabokov, and the Question of Translation

Does style in the novel, after all, count for much? Nabokov is an especially instructive test case because he is so clearly an exquisite, highly self-conscious stylist. He once claimed that he rewrote every sentence three or four times. The evidence on this question of style in the novel is in general somewhat mixed. A few prominent novelists, such as Dreiser, have been wretched stylists. Trollope's prose was no more than serviceable, yet with it he produced an abundance of genuinely engaging novels, a good many of which are fine representations of class and character in Victorian England. Balzac was not at all a brilliant stylist, and on occasion he could be bombastic, especially in his handling of figurative language, but *The Human Comedy* is among the most grand and enduring achievements of the genre. Stendhal famously announced that he wanted to fashion a factual, understated prose that would compete with the language of the civil registry, but style makes a real difference in his novels, and anyone who has read him in French is likely to sense a sad diminution of his lightness of touch and his worldly tone in the English translations. And at the other end of the field, many great novelists have been fine, and in some cases painstaking, stylists: Fielding (whom Stendhal greatly admired); Flaubert, the inaugurator of the modern idea of the novelist as fastidious artificer; Joyce, Kafka, and Nabokov, all of them varying heirs to the Flaubertian tradition; and, of course, Proust.

The question of style in the novel urgently needs to be addressed because it has been so widely neglected, especially in academic circles, for at least the past half-century. The principal reason for the neglect is quite evident: in departments of literary studies, the very term and concept of style—even of language itself—have been widely displaced by something called discourse, a notion that principally derives from Michel Foucault. Discourse in the sense that has generally been adopted is a manifestation, or perhaps rather a tool, of ideology. It flows through the circuits of society, manipulating individuals and groups in the interests of the powers that be, manifesting itself equally, or at least in related ways, in poetry and fiction, in political speeches, government directives, manuals of mental and physical hygiene, advertising, and much else. This orientation toward discourse was at the heart of the New Historicism (now a faded phenomenon), and it is instructive that one of its founders, Stephen Greenblatt, in the preface to his admirable *Hamlet in Purgatory*, should have felt constrained to say that there is no point in talking about Shakespeare if you do not respond to the magic of language, thus implicitly repudiating many of his followers and perhaps some of his own earlier inclinations.

After the New Historicism, though sometimes drawing on it, literary scholars have been busy pursuing a spectrum of purportedly political agendas with illustrative reference to literary texts—race, gender identity, sexual practices, the critique of colonialism, the excoriation of consumerism and of the evils of late capitalism and globalization. There has scarcely been room in such considerations for any attention to style—for the recognition that it is literary style which might make available to us certain precious perceptions of reality and certain distinctive pleasures not to be found elsewhere. When one encounters intelligent appreciations of style these days, they tend to come from practicing novelists, or from a few critics who have no more than one foot in academic life.

Against this background, *The Delighted States*, by Adam Thirlwell, a young British novelist, was a welcome engagement with unjustly marginalized issues that I will try to address in what follows.[1] The tenor of *The Delighted States* is nicely conveyed by the descriptive rubric, a grand flourish in eighteenth-century style, that is set beneath the title: "A Book of Novels, Romances, & Their Unknown Translators, Containing Ten Languages, Set on Four Continents, & Accompanied by Maps, Portraits, Squiggles, Illustrations, & a Variety of Helpful Indexes." The squiggles are mostly the ones that Sterne scatters through the pages of *Tristram Shandy* along with other typographical exuberances. The illustrations, which are part of the amusement of the book, consist mainly of photographs and portraits of the writers discussed, sometimes with friends and relations, and reproductions of the title pages of first editions of the novels. The conceit announced by Thirlwell for the presentation of these disparate materials is that this is not a work of criticism but itself a kind of novel: "This book—which I sometimes think of as a novel, an inside-out novel, with novelists as characters—is about the art of the novel. It is also, therefore, about the art of translation" (p. 8).

Although this claim to the status of novel is certainly inaccurate, it works well enough as a rhetorical ploy, inviting readers to imagine themselves in the pleasant company of one of those chatty, urbane, witty narrators who presided over novels from

Fielding (barely mentioned in the book) to Svevo and, still occasionally, beyond. I should say that Thirlwell's list of favorite novelists happily coincides to a large degree with my own, and most of the writers he discusses at length are ones I have been drawn to write about over the years: Cervantes, Sterne, Diderot, Stendhal, Flaubert, Joyce, Kafka, Nabokov, Bellow. It is clear from this list that he is especially interested in novelists who are playfully self-conscious about the art of the novel, who probe their relationship with their readers, flaunt the fictionality of their fictions, and call attention to the formal patterns of their artifice. Among recent novelists, it is Nabokov who preeminently displays all these features, and pride of place is accorded him in this book. Thirlwell also assumes, as he makes explicit at one point, that the novel is essentially a comic form. (Flaubert would not quite fit, but perhaps Kafka might, as a writer who at least in Walter Benjamin's view produced theological comedy.) What Thirlwell has to say about these sundry writers is for the most part perfectly apt, though not much of it will seem new to anybody familiar with the novels and with the criticism on them.

It is worth considering why a book on the art of the novel might also necessarily be a book on the art of translation, for this will bring us closer to the question of style that concerns us. Novels, rather more than poetry, have enjoyed the most vigorous international circulation in translation. Few of us read Russian, but Tolstoy and Dostoevsky loom large in the imaginative landscape of most people seriously interested in literature, even if their early experience of these writers was through the Edwardian tonalities and inaccuracies of Constance Garnett's English versions. What is even more remarkable is that many writers have been inspired by novelists whom they could not read in the original: the Brazilian Machado de Assis by Sterne and Fielding; the Yiddish writer Mendele Moykher Sforim by Cervantes; S. Y. Agnon by Knut Hamsun and Flaubert. Highly productive literary cross-fertilization has been consummated even when the translation used was seriously flawed, sometimes actually riddled with errors.

There is something scandalous about the manifest translatability of the novel, which might shed some light on the role of style in the novel. The principal purpose of Thirlwell's instructive study is to make sense of this scandal. He is finely sensitive to the way an assonance, an alliteration, a cadence, a subtle and surprising turn of syntax, shape our responses to what we read, and so he is led to puzzle over why so much of the translated novel seems to come through in the absence of most such refinements of style. Toward the end, he summarizes this central puzzlement: "All through this book, I have been arguing that style is the most important thing, and survives its mutilating translations—that although the history of translation is always a history of disillusion, somehow something survives. Yet this still shocks me, with my aesthetic prejudices, and preferences" (p. 429).

As an exemplary instance of the scandal of translatability, Thirlwell cites Bashevis Singer's spectacular success in American English, which was famously inaugurated in 1953 with Saul Bellow's translation of "Gimpel the Fool." Bellow's English version is captivatingly robust, but as Thirlwell notes, there is a small shift in meaning from the very first words: "I am Gimpel the fool. I don't think myself a fool" (p. 273). In the Yiddish, in the first sentence the word is *tam* and in the second sentence it is *nar*, with a nuance of difference between them. *Nar* (Germanic origin) is an out-and-out fool, whereas *tam* (Hebrew origin) suggests mental simplicity and perhaps innocence as well. As Singer then proceeded to collaborate with a variety of different translators, he himself was notoriously indifferent to such nuances, freely altering his Yiddish texts in the working sessions in the interest of making them more viable in English. "Singer's style," Thirlwell notes, "was able to accommodate quite a lot of loss and destruction. It was not the delicate thing that a style is meant to be" (p. 273). This is one of those cases where the extreme case teaches us something about the typical.

Flaubert's style was in fact a delicate thing, but still *Madame Bovary* in translation has been able to grip both general readers and other novelists, despite the fact that much of the delicacy is likely to have been effaced. This strong impact is less true of the translations of Flaubert's greatest novel, *Sentimental Education*. My guess is that the difference lies in the compelling story of self-delusion and self-destruction that carries *Madame Bovary* forward even without the fine turns of style, whereas *Sentimental Education* is purposefully a novel in which nothing happens, in which everything depends on the subtle representation of the protagonist's apprehension of society, the historical events that he witnesses, and the illusory realm of desire. Absent this stylistic finesse, what is beautifully shaded in the French may seem a little flat in translation.

Camus, in an essay called "*Problèmes du roman*" that Thirlwell cites, shrewdly remarked that "people imagine—wrongly—that novels do not require style. They do, in fact, demand style of the most difficult kind, the one which takes second place" (p. 430). Style in the novel is the most difficult kind because, even when the writer invests extravagant labor in it, ultimately it has to incorporate an element of self-abnegation: a novel in which style is the supreme end in itself runs the danger of devolving into preciosity or mannerism. But to what must style take second place? I think one would have to say (this is not what Thirlwell says) that it is the representation of the social, historical, and political world, and of the thoughts, emotions, and moral experiences of the characters.

Near the beginning of his book, Thirlwell proposes what looks like an antithetical view. All novels, he says, are "miniaturizations. They are never real life itself. Real life is always elsewhere" (p. 15). It is this very chasm between world and book, he goes on to argue, that makes translation possible: "The style of a novel, and a novelist, is a set of instructions, a project: it is never able to create an entirely unique, irreplaceable object" (p. 15). The question, of course, is what is the aim and nature of the project. Virtually all novels, whether they are as zany as *Tristram Shandy* or as obsessive as *Crime and Punishment* or as wittily self-conscious as *Pale Fire*, seek to create, I think, some imaginatively arresting simulacrum of the world that we more or less know, which is of course made up of things, events, people, relationships, and institutions, and not of words. Novelists have only language with which to construct their simulacra of the world. "Oh, my Lolita," Humbert Humbert famously says, expressing not only his own desperation in his prison cell but the ontological anxiety of every novelist, "I have only words to play with!"

"Miniaturization" is a clever way of designating this ontological gap between the novel and the world, but it is not quite right. A novel is always immeasurably smaller than its objects of representation—a life, a relationship, a city, a society, a historical moment—but its fundamental mimetic trick is precisely that it does not feel small. Through the artful deployment of a relatively limited number of words—say, one hundred thousand for a run-of-the-mill novel—the writer creates an illusion of the largeness of life. The novelistic use of language may legitimately be thought of as "a set of instructions, a project" that enables the reader to imagine a particular configuration of human experience, but such a characterization has one mislead-ing implication. Sets of instructions are not dependent on the medium in which they are formulated.

The instructions for assembling a chair you have been impru-dent enough to purchase from a catalog may be expressed in words or entirely in a series of diagrams, but if you successfully follow the instructions, you will end up with the same chair whether you have been guided by words or by pictures. Novels are just a little bit like this, which may be why they lend them-selves to translation. When Emma Bovary, after her first tryst with Rodolphe, deliriously tells herself, "I have a lover," the fact that "lover" sounds different from *amant* and might conceivably have slightly different cultural implications scarcely matters. Readers of the novel in translation get the essential idea that Flaubert meant to convey, including the social role referred to, the character's erotic excitement, and her romantic delusions, for which the words he chose serve as a set of instructions.

Yet something happens in the novel through the elaborately wrought medium of style that resists translation, even as the large, represented world of the novel is conveyed well enough in another language. If you try to imagine *Moby-Dick* in French or Chinese or Hindi, you can readily conceive that the tale of Ahab's monstrous monomania and of the exotic crew of the *Pequod*, the tremendous evocations of the great white whale as a virtually mythological presence, the vivid descriptions of the chase in small boats for whales, would all still come across to far-flung readers. And that is what style takes second place to in the novel. Still, it is a second place that has electrifying impor-tance. Consider even a brief sentence: "The sea was as a crucible of molten gold, that bubblingly leaps with light and heat."[2] A translation could easily reproduce the simile of the crucible of molten gold and the vigor of the verb "leaps," but the deliberate oddness of the adverbial "bubblingly" that focuses the movement of the water and the alliteration and assonance of "leaps with light and heat" that lock the clause together are another matter. All these small stylistic effects help create the lyric intensity of this moment of the sea perceived from the moving ship, and they are bound to be diminished in translation.

A different operation of the force of style may be seen in these words from a dramatic dialogue spoken by the black cabin-boy Pip: "Oh, thou big white God aloft there somewhere in yon darkness, have mercy on this small black boy down here; preserve him from all men that have no bowels to feel fear!"[3] The artful shaping of the language is less spectacular here, but it is no less decisive. The dense clustering of monosyllabic words generates a clenched power. Instead of any gesture toward African American dialect, Pip is made to speak a dignified poetic language that in its pronounced iambic cadences is reminiscent, like much else in this novel, of Shakespeare. The archaic "yon" is ancillary to this intention, and the use of "bowels" in the sense of "deep feelings" or "compassion," drawn directly from the King James Version of the Bible, equally harks back to the early seventeenth century. The high solemnity of Pip's address to God could presumably be conveyed in another language, but it is the specific biblical resonances (perhaps, especially, of Psalms) and of Shakespeare (as usual in this novel, ultimately pointing to *King Lear*) that give these words their peculiar metaphysical and poetic dignity, resisting translation.

Style is immensely important in the particular account of the art of the novel offered by Adam Thirlwell and of the art of translation, but it is hard to make out what, finally, he means by style. The chatty, episodic, sometimes free-associative expository strategy he uses, abounding in engaging anecdotes about novelists and translators, makes *The Delighted States* a charming book but not much of a vehicle for sustained thought. What we get is a scattering of pronouncements on style, often tending toward aphorism, and not obviously linked together in a single conceptual frame. "A style, in the end, is a list of methods by which a novelist achieves various effects" (p. 20). Well, yes, but what does this banality tell us that we didn't already know? Or: "No art work is ever the thing itself. It is always inflected by a style" (p. 195). Fair enough, though this is rather like reminding us that in a painting, oils on canvas are used to represent a certain perception of a three-dimensional object in two dimensions and are not the thing itself. And finally: "A style is not just a prose style. Sometimes, it is not even a form of composition. Style is a quality of vision; a soul" (p. 308). One has to assent to this declaration, furlongs distant as it may be from the definition of style as a list of methods. A quality of vision is surely what defines the small specimens of Melville's style that I have just cited. But is there any way to speak cogently about this quality of vision and to consider to what degree it may be wedded to the original language in which it is cast?

Consider the case of Dickens, who is surely the most energetically original stylist among nineteenth-century British novelists (and who, weirdly, barely figures in *The Delighted States*). Now, the novels of Dickens have enjoyed the most prominent international currency in a variety of languages—Russian, German, Yiddish, Hebrew, and many others. One can see how the elaborate plots with their ingenious resolutions, the wild humor, the vivid caricatures, the brilliant metaphors, might all be conveyed in other languages. But Dickens is a master of mesmerizing cadences and subtle shifts in linguistic register, of sound-play and allusive echoes—all of which constitute the quality of vision that is his ultimately untranslatable style. It is noteworthy that Nabokov the great stylist singles out Dickens's style for unstinting admiration in his *Lectures on Literature*, as we have seen. Here is a moment from the last completed novel by Dickens, *Our Mutual Friend*, in which the young (and rather colorless) heroine steps outside the door of a ramshackle pub in a seedy neighborhood along the Thames:

> The chaining of the door behind her, as she went forth, disenchanted Lizzie Hexam of that first relief she had felt. The night was black and shrill, the river-side wilderness was melancholy, and there was a sound of casting-out, in the rattling of iron links, and the grating of the bolts and staples under Miss Abbey's hand. As she came beneath the lowering sky, a sense of being involved in a murky shade of Murder dropped upon her; and, as the tidal swell of the river broke at her feet without her seeing how it gathered, so her thoughts startled her by rushing out of an unseen void and striking at her heart.

The only translations I have been able to locate are one in Russian and one done in 1954 in French by a team of three translators, to which I will refer. (The international canon has evidently embraced *Oliver Twist* and *David Copperfield* but not *Our Mutual Friend*.) One might characterize this representation of Lizzie stepping out into the menacing London night while the door is bolted behind her as a moment of high melodrama, though it is a melodrama that, through the agency of Dickens's style, assumes the potency of myth. The metallic clanging and rattling of those chains and bolts that shut Lizzie out in the realm of darkness are what palpably pull the scene together, and these can be conveyed by a competent translation, as the French trio demonstrate. But the sound of the language and the resonance of certain key terms are something else. Like Melville, though without the intention of invoking Shakespeare and Milton, Dickens gives his prose the enchantment of poetry by repeatedly gliding into iambic cadences: "The night was black and shrill"; "she came beneath the lowering sky"; "and striking at her heart." He beautifully counterpoints insistent monosyllabic words ("night," "black," "shrill") with polysyllabic ones ("wilderness," "melancholy"). The French turns all this into something that sounds vaguely like the flaccid Romantic poetry of Lamartine: *La nuit était noire, la bise perçante, la rive déserte et morne*. The inspired choice of the term "casting-out" brings the entire passage into the eschatological orbit of the New Testament's "cast[ing] out into" a place of "wailing and gnashing of teeth." The phonetic assimilation of "murky" and "Murder" has the effect of coagulating the thickening sense of terror that informs the scene. (The French entirely throws in the towel here, dispensing with the expected *ténébreux* for "murky" and blandly saying that Lizzie felt above her *une atmosphère de meurtre*.) Against this whole ominous background, the "unseen void" at the end takes on cosmic amplitude—"void" is, after all, the world that the King James Version chose for the chaos before creation at the beginning of Genesis—while the parallel structure that locks "void" in with "heart" makes a grand climax to this experience of midnight dread.

There is no process more instructive about the subtle articulations and the intricate semantic layering of a literary text than the attempt to translate it. The process is a humbling one, as any honest translator will confess. The scandalous fact that so much of the original manages to get through, for all the reshapings and misshapings that a translator inevitably inflicts on the author's words, is a happy circumstance for anyone who loves literature: despite the linguistic ignorance we share, we may enjoy the literary riches of other cultures, imperfect as that enjoyment may often be. At the same time, the gap between even a very good translation—Thirlwell provides an excellent one of the initial French version of Nabokov's "Mademoiselle O" as an appendix to his book—and the original reminds us that style plays a determinative role in constituting the imaginative world of any work of fiction. In fact, one of the reasons for the sense of largeness in the represented world of a good novel is, as the few examples I have offered illustrate, that the sundry components of language are made to fit together in a way that creates the sense of an integrated world, not merely of bits and pieces of narrative and of descriptive detail.

This stylistic integration, by and large, is performed intuitively and not by calculation, though there have been some fanatically calculating stylists, such as Flaubert and Joyce, to whom one surely can add Nabokov. Language comprises highly heterogeneous elements, so the constituents of style are themselves heterogeneous and their combinations and permutations intrinsically unpredictable. The sound and the length of the words, their syntactic ordering, the cadences in which they are arranged, the levels of diction they manifest, the antecedent texts they evoke explicitly or obliquely, their deployment of figurative language—all combine in shifting patterns to put an indelible stamp on one moment after another and on the entire fictional world constituted from those moments. Reading the untranslatable text is ultimately what departments of literary studies ought to be about, but in the pseudopolitical atmosphere that has dominated the academy for several decades, the reverse has taken place: the original text has been read as though it might as well have been a translation. Teachers of literature and their hapless students have tended to look right through style to the purported grounding of the text in one ideology or another.

The double lesson of translation is that style does not mean everything in a work of literature but that it means a great deal, and certainly more than translation can convey. Great literature, any sensitive reader will grant, is in some way a magical thing, and this magic is not only a process of inducing rapture but also of enabling thought, inviting the perception of complex associative links, seeing one frame of meaning in connection with another, or with several others. Attending to style is intensely pleasurable and, in the best cases, illuminating as well.

The relation between style and translation is tested in an anomalous way in Nabokov's fiction. He grew up in prerevolutionary Russia with three languages and claimed that the three were all virtually native, although Russian was clearly his first great love. Until 1938, all his novels, constituting roughly half of his total production, were written in Russian during his exile in Berlin and Paris. He translated two of these himself into English in the 1930s. Most of the remaining Russian novels were turned into English by his son Dimitri in the 1960s, but with the collaboration of the author. Nabokov certainly had some reservations about his early Russian writing, and in the foreword to the English version of *Despair*, a translation done without the assistance of Dimitri, he observed of himself, "he has nothing but impatience for the bungling apprentice of his youth." These translations, then, are in varying degrees reworkings of the Russian originals that to some extent reflect certain procedures Nabokov had perfected over a quarter of a century as an English novelist. As such, they involve issues different from the kind of chasm between the original and the translation that one readily sees, say, in the French or other versions of *Our Mutual Friend*, *Moby-Dick*, and virtually all remarkable novels that revel in the distinctive resources of the English language. In any event, I lack the linguistic competence to examine the sometimes extensive transformations of the Russian Nabokov by the English Nabokov—though with this last adjective I refer only to the language, for one should note that he preferred to represent himself as an "American novelist"—so I shall proceed to consider two very different passages from his novels composed in English in order to get some sense of what is achieved through style in his fiction.

One of the rapturous moments in *Lolita* is Humbert Humbert's vision of Lolita playing tennis. In the first-person narrative, his evocation of Lolita wielding her racket is a memory, not a report synchronic with the action:

> The exquisite clarity of all her movements had its auditory counterpart in the pure ringing sound of every stroke. The ball when it entered her aura of control became somewhat whiter, its resilience somehow richer, and the instrument of precision she used on it seemed inordinately prehensile and deliberate at the moment of clinging contact. . . . I remember at the very first game I watched being drenched with an almost painful convulsion of beauty assimilation. My Lolita had a way of raising her bent left knee at the ample and springy start of a service cycle when there would develop and hang in the sun for a second a vital web of balance between toed foot, pristine armpit, burnished arm and far back-flung racket, as she smiled up with gleaming teeth at the small globe suspended so high in the zenith of the powerful and graceful cosmos she had created for the express purpose of falling upon it with a clear resounding crack of her golden whip. (pp. 231–232)

The passage is a remarkable blend of erotic obsession and a lover's lyric celebration of the object of his love, although the latter is more salient here. One of the moral complexities of *Lolita*, as I noted in my chapter on that novel, is the protagonist's manifestly perverted sexual fixation on a prepubescent child turning into genuine love, with the love leading Humbert Humbert by the end of the novel to the remorseful realization of how he has robbed Lolita of her childhood by his sexual abuse of her. This tricky balance between Humbert the lover and Humbert the pervert, which I looked at more closely earlier, is, as one sees here, realized through the fine articulation of language.

One hallmark of Nabokov's style is a certain element of surprise in his word choice. "Exquisite clarity" is not an attribute ordinarily associated with athletic movement. "Prehensile" for the contact of racket with ball is still more surprising, though once having been stated, it seems perfectly right. "Aura" in the context of racket swing is equally unanticipated but will be picked up by related terms later in the passage. Humbert Humbert remembers, when he first watched Lolita on the court, his "being drenched with an almost painful convulsion of beauty assimilation." The strategic choice of words virtually suggests a violently intense ejaculation in the excitement of beholding Lolita at play on the court, but the final phrase, "of beauty assimilation," may pull the reader back from this explicitly physiological reading and lead one to conclude instead that the sexual hint is primarily a submerged metaphor for the aesthetic ecstasy that this entranced observer experiences. Nabokov, we should remember, was an avid and skillful tennis player, and thus all the details of the service motion are precisely represented, but they are also transmuted into a kind of myth. The "pristine armpit" Lolita exposes as she lifts her racket to serve is of course an indication that the twelve-year-old girl has not yet gone through puberty, and so it is a reflection of Humbert's perversion in the midst of all this lyric celebration. "Pristine" is perfectly chosen—"bare" would not have worked in the same way because the word Nabokov uses reflects his protagonist's sexual bondage to prepubescent girls as the only viable objects of desire. But the pristine armpit is also coordinated with the "burnished arm"—presumably, both smooth and suntanned—that helps to make Lolita seem rather like the statue of some Greek goddess in motion. That effect is reinforced at the end of this excerpt by the transformation of the racket into a "golden whip," and the server's swing is endowed with mythic amplitude by the representation of the tennis ball as a "small globe" and the calculated height of her toss as "the zenith of the powerful and graceful cosmos she had created." The perfect balance of style with its artful deployment of metaphorical elements in this way sets Humbert Humbert's rapture over Lolita in a tradition of lyric celebrations of the beloved that goes back to Renaissance poetry, without altogether letting us forget that his obsession with her is twisted and morally repugnant. It should be kept in mind that more than once in his interviews, Nabokov said that he thought of Humbert as a monster.

To revert to the question of the translatability of style in the novel, a brief comparison with a French version of the passage may be instructive. The admirable French translation is by Maurice Couturier, the dean of Nabokov scholars in France. I would say that only a little is lost in the transfer of Nabokov's virtuosic English into Couturier's apt French. The success of the translation is testimony to why so many novels work well in other languages—why, for example, we readers without Russian can relish Tolstoy's brilliance even though we no doubt miss many things visible only to someone reading the original. I would add that Nabokov may be more amenable to rendering in French than such novelists as Faulkner, Melville, and Dickens, who play extravagantly with the different registers of the English language, because he taps a French tradition of style in the novel as perfectly wrought artifice that goes back to Flaubert.

Nevertheless, there are a few fine touches in the English that don't quite make it into the French. I will mention just four. The remarkable "drenched with an almost painful convulsion of beauty assimilation" becomes *submergé par un spasme de plénitude esthétique presque douloureux.* Perhaps Couturier's ear as a native speaker led him to feel that the obvious French equivalent for "drenched," *trempé,* didn't sound right, but "submerged" loses the archly oblique suggestion of sexual release of the English. "*Plénitude esthétique*" is actually more elegant than Nabokov's "beauty assimilation," though it lacks the nuance of bodily absorption of the English. The wonderful "pristine armpit" becomes *cette aiselle immaculée* because there is no good French equivalent for "pristine," but this loses something of Humbert Humbert's fixation on prepubescence. Nabokov's neat little innovation of "toed foot" becomes *ce pied dressé sur sa pointe,* probably a bit too balletic, but there is no way of creating a French equivalent of the little invention "toed." Finally as a matter of rhythm and syntactic position at the very end of this paragraph: "her golden whip" has to be in French *sa cravache d'or* (although because *cravache* is specifically a riding-whip, *fouet* might have been used), which slightly dilutes the effect of climactically concluding the paragraph on the semantically sharp, rhythmically emphatic monosyllable "whip."[4]

All these, I hasten to say, are rather minor losses in the translation. What Couturier's skillful representation of Nabokov's prose in French demonstrates is that certain kinds of style in the novel, including even a style so consciously wrought and so inventive as Nabokov's, can survive quite nicely in the migration from language to language, provided the translator is sensitive to the original and has a good stylistic control of his or her own language.

Let us now consider a passage from Nabokov in which a riot of metaphor predominates. Pnin, in the novel to which he gives his name, the endearing émigré professor constantly struggling with his colleagues, with his students, and with the mysteries of the English language, has just undergone the ordeal of having all his crumbling teeth extracted:

> A warm flow of pain was gradually replacing the ice and wood of the anesthetic in his thawing, still half-dead, abominably martyred mouth. After that, for a few days, he was in mourning for an intimate part of himself. It surprised him to realize how fond he had been of his teeth. His tongue, a flat sleek seal, used to flop and slide so happily among the familiar rocks, checking the contours of a battered but still secure kingdom, plunging from cave to cove, climbing this jag, nuzzling that notch, finding a shred of sweet seaweed in the same old cleft; but now not a landmark remained, and all there existed was a great dark wound, a terra incognita of gums which dread and disgust forbade one to investigate. And when the plates were thrust in, it was like a poor fossil skull being fitted with the jaws of a perfect stranger. (p. 38)

Pnin is not a first-person narrative like *Lolita;* rather, its story is told by what amounts to a clandestine narrator. As we saw in the chapter on *Pnin,* at first he seems like a more or less traditional novelistic omniscient narrator, but through a few early hints and by gradual stages he gives himself away as a character—a successful émigré novelist, a kind of negative double of Nabokov (he is even a lepidopterist), a man who has had an affair with the woman who was married to Pnin and heartlessly discarded her, driving her to attempt suicide, a person generally condescending but sometimes sympathetic to Pnin. In the dental disaster represented in our passage, sympathy prevails.

In regard to the pesky criterion of translatability, many of the stylistic details in the quoted passage could readily be conveyed in another language because the inventive deployment of metaphor is so central. As we've seen elsewhere, Nabokov liked to speak, a bit provocatively but quite seriously, about the precision of poetry and the rapture of science, and his poetic prose in this instance is remarkable for its precision in representing the ghastly experience of a total dental extraction. The "ice and wood of the anesthetic" fading into postoperative pain expresses with poetic precision the physical sensation most of us have known after the extraction of even a single tooth. The narrator's "It surprised him to realize how fond he had been of his teeth" is a witty, slightly amusing formulation—this is a narrator who often chooses to be amused by Pnin's sundry plights—that nevertheless nicely suggests poor Pnin's feeling of dismay. The wounded mouth is then transformed through figurative language into a lively landscape by the sea, the tongue "a flat sleek seal," the eroding teeth jagged rocks, the remnants of food stuck between them "sweet seaweed." One should keep in mind that in any finely wrought writing, not only the meaning of words and the images that they mark are important but also their sound and shape (a feature that is more of a challenge to translate). Note the predominance of monosyllabic words in the passage—"tongue," "flat sleek seal," "flop and slide," "shred," "cave to cove" (which is also a strong alliteration), "jag," "notch," "cleft." The use of "jag" not in its conventional sense of "binge" (as, for example, "an eating jag") is an ad hoc innovation of Nabokov's, obviously indicating a "jagged place" and coined to serve the purposes of the integrated monosyllabic scene. Does sound have meaning? a reader may well ask. Not really, of course, but as the literary theorist Benjamin Harshav observed long ago, what a pattern of interrelated sounds can do is to underscore the semantic content of the words and give any particular moment in a literary representation a sense of emphasis and interwoven wholeness. In our passage all the details of the tongue exploring the uneven surfaces of the hard if decaying teeth are tightly interlinked both through the governing metaphor of the mouth as rocky seashore and the pattern of related sounds.

What should be equally noted is the sheer exuberance in the play of metaphor in all its force of mimetic precision. Nabokov repeatedly proposed in his *Lectures on Literature* and elsewhere that fiction should exert enchantment for the reader. His high esteem for enchantment may explain in part his entrenched prejudice against novelists he perceived to be merely earnest preachers of philosophical or moral ideas, the long list of his proscribed writers ranging from Conrad and Thomas Mann to Sartre and Camus. Playfulness is always an essential element of his fiction, manifested in his fondness for word games and coded signals and cunning literary allusions but perhaps above all in the elegant shapeliness and invented zest of his style. The concluding figurative term of our passage is still another instance of the writer at play in the fields of language and similitude: "it was like a poor fossil skull being fitted with the jaws of a perfect stranger." There is something macabre as well as amusing about this simile representing Pnin's feeling of alienation from the dental plates inserted in his recently excavated mouth, while it also exhibits that precision of poetry in conveying the concreteness of a very disorienting experience.

Is all this translatable? Let me briefly observe what happens to our passage in a German translation. The German is generally quite faithful to the lexical values of the English. The translator also makes some effort to reproduce Nabokov's sound-play. Thus, "from cave to cove" becomes *jener Grotte in dieser Grube,* and "climbing this jag, nuzzling that notch" is approximated, a bit less successfully, by *hatte jene Klippe erklommen, in dieser Kluft gestörbert.*[5] *Klippe / Kluft* is apt, but *hatte erklommen* for "nuzzling the notch" not only loses the alliteration but shifts the sense of intimate physical contact because the German verb suggests something like "to scale." The more pervasive disparity between the original and the translation has to do with a structural difference between the two languages. German does not lend itself to the same compactness that English does, and it is hard to reproduce in German the string of monosyllabic words that Nabokov uses so effectively here. An exemplary instance is the amusing "slop and slide happily among the familiar rocks," which in the German, perhaps because there is no other way to do it, is a polysyllabic plod: *so glücklich zwischen den vertrauten Klippen umhergesprungen und -geglitten.* A German reader will very likely enjoy most of the liveliness of the passage, but some of the enchantment of the prose effected through the inventive play of sound will have vanished.

Through all this, one can see how style in the novel can generate an intrinsic delighting momentum even as it performs an arresting function in imaginatively realizing experience, poiesis and mimesis nicely interfused. The two passages we have considered suggest something of the wide range of ends that style in the novel can serve. Lolita on the tennis court is a peak moment of lyric celebration that also focuses a decisive aspect of the protagonist's imagination and psychology. The painful comedy enacted through metaphors representing Pnin's ravaged mouth is both touching and amusing, but it is no more than another instance of his haplessness and surely not some central nexus of theme and character in this particular novel. Yet in both instances, it is style that engages the reader and gives amplitude and strong presence to the vividly realized moment of the protagonist's experience.

Our exploration of how translatable all this could be tells us something about the role of style in the novel and the limits of that role. Style determines a great deal of what happens in a novel but not quite everything. Some styles in fiction, as I have noted, are not easily exportable to another language and culture because they embody, too extravagantly, idiosyncratic deployments of the language in which they were written. Nabokov as consummate stylist is constantly resourceful and often surprising in what he does with the English language, but perhaps because his prose is so finely polished, much of it manages to come across in the hands of an adept translator. There remains nevertheless an element of distinctively Nabokovian allure wrought through his use of English—"the slop and slide" of the "fat sleek seal"; the vital web of balance between "toed foot, pristine armpit, burnished arm and far-flung racket"—that does not cross the barrier of translation. Those of us who are fortunate enough to read him in his original language, as in a perfect literary utopia we would read all novels, should be grateful for this gift. The stylistic elegance and inventiveness of Nabokov's fiction are clearly a key element in our enjoyment as readers, but they also contribute in innumerable ways to our vision of character, setting, and moral predicament.

NOTES

Chapter 1. Between Appreciation and Defense

1. Mark Lilly, "Nabokov: Homo Ludens," in *Vladimir Nabokov: A Tribute*, ed. Peter Quennell (London: Weidenfeld & Nicolson, 1979), p. 89.

2. *The Stories of Vladimir Nabokov* (New York: Alfred A. Knopf, 1995), p. 564. All subsequent references, with page numbers in the body of the text, are to this edition.

Chapter 2. Not Reading the Papers

1. Quoted in Brian Boyd, *Vladimir Nabokov: The Russian Years* (Princeton, NJ: Princeton University Press, 1990), p. 409.

2. Boyd, *Vladimir Nabokov*, p. 82.

3. Viktor Shklovsky, "Art as Technique," in *Russian Formalist Criticism: Four Essays*, edited by L. T. Lemon and M. J. Reis (Lincoln: University of Nebraska Press, 1965), p. 12.

4. Vladimir Nabokov, *King, Queen, Knave* (New York: McGraw-Hill, 1968), p. 9.

5. Vladimir Nabokov, *Bend Sinister* (New York: Time, 1964), p. 54.

Chapter 3. *Lolita* Now

1. *The Annotated Lolita*, edited by Alfred Appel Jr., revised edition (New York: Vintage Books, 1991), p. 49. All subsequent quotations from *Lolita* and from the annotations are from this edition.

Chapter 4. Nabokov's Game of Worlds

1. Vladimir Nabokov, *Pale Fire* (New York: Putnam, 1962), p. 22. All subsequent quotations are from this edition.

2. Vladimir Nabokov, *Poems and Problems* (New York: McGraw-Hill, 1970), pp. 159–160.

Chapter 5. Autobiography as Alchemy in *Pale Fire*

1. Vladimir Nabokov, *Strong Opinions* (New York: McGraw-Hill, 1973), p. 95.

Chapter 6. *Ada*, or the Perils of Paradise

1. Vladimir Nabokov, *Ada* (New York: McGraw-Hill, 1969), p. 89. All subsequent quotations are from this edition.

2. Ellen Pifer, *Nabokov and the Novel* (Cambridge, MA: Harvard University Press), 1980.

Chapter 7. Nabokov for Those Who Hate Him

1. Vladimir Nabokov, *Pnin* (New York: Random House/Vintage, 1989), p. 101. All subsequent quotations are from this edition.

2. Gennady Barabtarlo, *Phantom of Fact: A Guide to Nabokov's "Pnin"* (Ann Arbor, MI: Ardis, 1989).

3. Eric Naiman, *Nabokov Perversely* (Ithaca, NY: Cornell University Press, 2010), pp. 74–104.

4. Roland Barthes, "The Reality Effect," in *French Literary Theory Today*, edited by Tzvetan Todorov (Cambridge, UK: Cambridge University Press, 1982), pp. 11–17.

5. Viktor Shklovsky, "Sterne's *Tristram Shandy:* Stylistic Commentary," in *Russian Formalist Criticism: Four Essays*, edited by L. T. Lemon and Marion J. Reis (Lincoln: University of Nebraska Press, 1965), p. 57.

Chapter 8. *Invitation to a Beheading*

1. Simon Karlinsky, "Illusion, Reality, and Parody in Nabokov's Plays," *Wisconsin Studies in Contemporary Literature* 8, no. 2 (Spring 1967), p. 268.

2. Vladimir Nabokov, *Invitation to a Beheading* (New York: Capricorn Books, 1959), p. 12. All subsequent quotations are from this edition.

3. Vladimir Nabokov, *The Gift* (New York: G. P. Putnam, 1963), p. 215.

4. Julian Moynihan, "A Russian Preface to Nabokov's *Beheading*," *Novel* 1, no. 1 (Fall 1967), p. 16.

5. Vladimir Nabokov, *Nikolai Gogol* (Norfolk, CT: New Directions, 1944), p. 65.

Chapter 9. Nabokov and Memory

1. Vladimir Nabokov, *Speak, Memory* (New York: G. P. Putnam, 1966), pp. 308–309. All subsequent quotations are from this edition.

Chapter 10. Lectures on Literature

1. Vladimir Nabokov, *Lectures on Literature*, edited by Fredson Bowers (New York: Harcourt Brace Jovanovich, 1980). All subsequent quotations are from this edition.

Chapter 11. Style in the Novel, Style in Nabokov, and the Question of Translation

1. Adam Thirlwell, *The Delighted States* (New York: Farrar, Straus and Giroux, 2007). All subsequent quotations are from this edition.

2. Herman Melville, *Moby-Dick*, Norton Critical Edition, edited by Harrison Hayford and Hershel Parker (New York: W. W. Norton, 1967), p. 423.

3. Melville, *Moby-Dick*, p. 108.

4. Vladimir Nabokov, *Oeuvres romanesques complètes*, translated by Maurice Couturier, vol. 2 (Paris: Gallimard, 2010), pp. 1051–1052.

5. Vladimir Nabokov, *Pnin*, vol. 9 of *Gesammelte Werke*, translated by Dieter Zimmer (Hamburg: Rowohlt, 1999), p. 45.

SOURCES

Chapters 1 ("Between Appreciation and Defense") and 3 ("*Lolita* Now") are new essays written for this book. The other chapters originally appeared as follows:

Chapter 2, "Not Reading the Papers," adapted and expanded from "Tyrants and Butterflies," *The New Republic*, Oct. 15, 1990.

Chapter 4, "Nabokov's Game of Worlds," from my book *Partial Magic: The Novel as a Self-Conscious Genre* (Berkeley: University of California Press, 1975).

Chapter 5, "Autobiography as Alchemy in *Pale Fire*," *Cycnos* 10, no. 1 (1983) (Nice, France).

Chapter 6, "*Ada*, or the Perils of Paradise," from *Nabokov: A Tribute*, edited by Peter Quennell (London: Weidenfeld & Nicolson, 1979).

Chapter 7, "Nabokov for Those Who Hate Him," from *Nabokov Upside Down*, edited by Brian Boyd and Marijeta Bedovic (Evanston, IL: Northwestern University Press, 2017).

Chapter 8, "*Invitation to a Beheading:* Nabokov and the Art of Politics," *TriQuarterly* 17 (Winter 1970).

Chapter 9, "Nabokov and Memory," *Partisan Review* 58, no. 2 (Fall 1991).

Chapter 10, "Lectures on Literature," adapted and expanded from "Nabokov's Lectures on Literature," *The New Republic*, Oct. 4, 1980.

Chapter 11, "Style in the Novel, Style in Nabokov, and the Question of Translation," adapted and expanded from "Only Words to Play With," *The New Republic*, June 25, 2008.

INDEX

A NOTE ON THE TYPE

This book has been composed in Arno, an Old-style serif typeface in the classic Venetian tradition, designed by Robert Slimbach at Adobe.